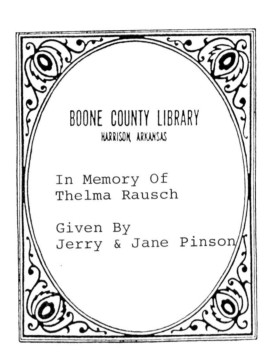

Breeding New Plants and Flowers

Charles W. Welch

The Crowood Press

First published in 2002 by
The Crowood Press Ltd
Ramsbury, Marlborough
Wiltshire SN8 2HR

British Library Cataloguing-in-Publication Data

A catalogue record for this book is available from the British Library.

ISBN 1 86126 549 2

Acknowledgements
I would like to thank Carol, my beloved wife, for putting up with my constantly requesting help in holding this plant or that flower, also for her opinion as to which would be her preferred colour, and her point of view regarding the varied scents of flowers that would appeal to the fairer sex.

Special thanks go to the customers of my previous restaurant for giving their qualified judgement on the flavour of the home-bred fruits served to them. They applied a one to ten marking, and helped in the process of producing some wonderful fruit varieties.

Line-drawings by author.

Photograph previous page: lupins.

Typeset and designed by
D & N Publishing
Baydon, Wiltshire.

Typeface used: M Plantin.

Printed and bound by Times Offset (M) Sdn. Bhd.

Contents

Introduction   5

Flowers   16
African Violets   16
Aquilegias   20
Begonias   24
Chrysanthemums   27
Clematis   31
Daffodils and Tulips   35
Dahlias   39
Delphiniums   43
Fuchsias   49
Gladioli   54
Heathers   58
Irises   63
Lilies   67
Lupins   73
Pansies and Violas   77
Pelargoniums (Geraniums)   82
Phlox   86
Pinks and Carnations   89
Primulas   95
Roses   100
Sweet Peas   105

Fruit and Vegetables   111
Potatoes   111
Tomatoes   115
Strawberries   120
Soft Fruits   125
Heathland Berries   130
Red-, Black- and Whitecurrants, and Gooseberries   131
Hard Fruits   134
Vegetables   138

Shrubs   140
Index   142

Cross between
cowslip × primrose.

Introduction

Every new season the seed and plant nurseries send out their catalogues hoping to tempt the public into buying their wares. Glossy, high quality pictures show the flowers to perfection in ideal conditions, and full instructions are given on how to achieve the same results. The introduction of new flowers, and plants in general, never fails to create interest. We are all tempted to add to our collections the latest varieties that we see exhibited in beautiful pictures, accompanied by a persuading write-up. These new varieties are of particular interest to the seed and plant nurseries as they undoubtedly give extra special value to their catalogues and help to attract customers. An amazing number of new plants arrives each year, adding to the thousands already on the market – but then many that have been around for some years are dropped.

New plants are always given priority over older varieties, with only the very best keeping a foothold. But not all new plants are winners, and unless they have staying power, hardiness and general appeal, they too will be dropped. The greatest satisfaction to a plant breeder is to see his creations still on sale to the general public many years after their introduction. The urge to improve on the existing plants becomes even stronger with initial success, and the keen, experienced eye looks for special qualities to fix in the genetic make-up of the new variety: because there is always room for advancement, each little amendment adds towards perfection.

Since the world began there has been a natural evolution, with change and adaptation involving all kinds of life, whether animal or plant. As the environment changes life forms must adapt, and any living thing unable to do so will not survive. It is because the ability to adapt is a part of every species that certain varieties can successfully survive changing conditions, and it is because of this quality that we can manipulate nature into producing the type of plants that we want. Furthermore, natural progressive evolution is usually a slow but sure process – but we hope to accomplish very similar or more dramatic changes in a much shorter time by our methods of cross-breeding.

PLANT ORIGINS

In times of early domestication, when crops were grown to provide food for man's families, a type of natural selection was employed to produce better crops for the following years. Unless the best seed from the finest crops was used in continuity, yields would deteriorate. Selection of the best would, as seasons go by, improve both quality and quantity, and very soon selective breeding would be under way. When only the best plants are grown, good quality material is forthcoming as a result of cross-pollination by the insects or self-pollination by the plants themselves, depending on the type of plant selected by the grower.

This method of selective growing has been the mainstay of man's activities for thousands of years. It is only in the last hundred years or less, which is recent compared to the time involved, that pollination induced by man has caused the breeding of plants to attain the high level of today. When used in conjunction with selection, this method is highly efficient, even though so far it can be considered only a beginning.

Scientific advances in plant breeding have played a significant part in sustaining the high quality of food production in all parts of the world. Many companies specialize in plant genetics, not only to produce something new, but also to improve on already highly developed plant life.

Rice crops, the main source of food in the Far East, have been developed to produce three crops per year instead of the usual two, each giving higher yields of the finest quality. The quality of sugar-beet today has made the UK self-sufficient, so that there is less reliance on sugar cane from abroad as compared to days gone by. Sweetcorn can be grown by the local gardener, almost an impossibility a few years ago – and all these varieties and many thousands more were created by cross-breeding manipulations by man.

Other changes are the result of mutations that occur naturally from time to time: for instance, when there is a change in the chromosome count, causing the plant to develop different genetic variations that could affect any part of the structure or development. These changes can bring about a different flower colour or leaf shape or some other characteristic alteration, and this is one aspect of plant breeding that is a great asset, as long as the change – even though it may appear to be of little significance – can be used to advantage and incorporated into the system, and thereby helps towards improvement.

Modern Methods

These genetic changes can be induced with modern methods of genetic engineering, by applying chemicals, heat or radiation, particularly to the bud in the leaf axil at an early stage of development. The genetic structure of all plants is based on a considerable number of genes that are held in construction, being joined in methodical order to produce long strands called chromosomes. Each gene has a specific role to play in creating the final plant, one that will be relative to the construction of the gene formation of that particular species.

Crossing two plants of the same species but from different environments will, in the process of fertilization, start the procedure to blend the genes, so creating a new structure of chromosomes. This course of action will create a family of seedlings, each with a combination of characteristics different from its sister seedlings, so that no two are exactly alike. Once such an outcross is used, then the variation of the genetic make-up of the seedlings is very complex, and many combinations are apparent. But, if a cross were then made between two sister

Sometimes freak flowers appear.

plants, the variation would be much less obvious, reducing the variability in characteristics.

When two plants from pure lines are cross-pollinated, the dominant genes come to the fore: thus if red is the dominant colour, then all the seedlings will be of the same red hue. If, on the other hand, one plant is blue and the other red, when cross-pollinated the most dominant of the two colours would still take preference, and all the plant offspring would show the dominant colour. However, although 50 per cent of these red plants would be true red plants, the other 50 per cent would be showing red flowers, but their genetic make-up would be such that half the colour genes would be dominant red, and the other half recessive blue.

To produce a blue plant with some of the red plant's attributes, two plants possessing the recessive blue genes must be crossed with each other to produce 25 per cent pure red, 50 per cent red + blue, but also 25 per cent pure blue (which was the reason for the cross). All these blues incidentally will be pure blue, and if crossed with each other would again produce pure blues. Unfortunately there is no way of knowing which red plant has the blue recessive gene, and only by crossing different red seedlings from the red × blue cross, and keeping records of each to isolate the ones that produce the blue flower, will you have a variety of plants to select with the qualities of the red plant with the blue colour, or *vice versa*.

This is the basic method with which to start plant breeding, and success will depend on a certain amount of luck; but knowledge of genetics, even on a small scale, is a vital ingredient in the route to perfection.

FLOWER TYPES

There are so many different flower types that we will start by selecting the most popular. Although the range is huge, most plants in fact have the same method of reproduction and can come under the same method of manipulation.

The best way to understand the make-up of a flower and to study the sexual parts in detail, is to dissect it by pulling the bloom apart petal by petal until the stigma and stamens are exposed. When a variety of plants has been examined, it becomes obvious that they all have the same method of reproduction, but each uses a different approach. Many, such as the lily, the gladiolus and a number of other bell-type flowers, are quite simple, and

'Blushing Moon', best seedling iris at Wisley Iris Show 2001.

even the more complicated ones – the chrysanthemum, sweet pea and iris – which look quite daunting are, once stripped down, in fact quite similar, their differences easy to overcome. The majority of plants in this cross-breeding programme will fall into two categories. One is 'sexual', whereby seeds are sown to develop a plant that can only be propagated by the same type of plant, so developing more seed to perpetuate the family; this will include most annuals. The second category might be termed 'asexual': these types are grown from seeds initially, but the identical line is supplied either by cuttings, as with fuchsias, chrysanthemums and the like, or by runners, as with strawberries.

POLLEN

Pollen grains are the key to unlocking the treasures we hope to create, but first the way in which to apply them must be established – and not only how to administer the perfectly ripe pollen to the receptive stigma, but when, which can make the difference between success and failure.

Pollen grains are almost as variable as grains of dust, although many variations are well known and

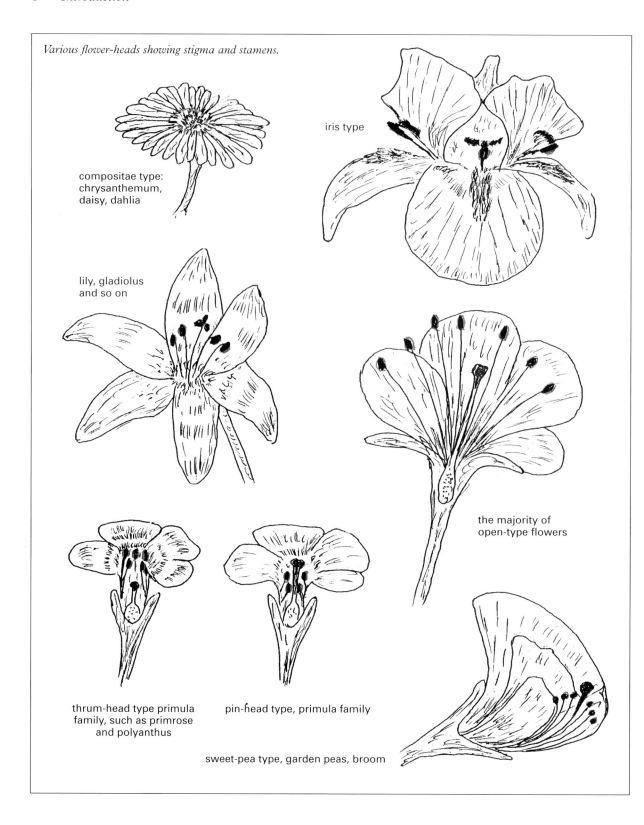

Various flower-heads showing stigma and stamens.

iris type

compositae type:
chrysanthemum,
daisy, dahlia

lily, gladiolus
and so on

the majority of
open-type flowers

thrum-head type primula
family, such as primrose
and polyanthus

pin-head type, primula family

sweet-pea type, garden peas, broom

pollen; to achieve this, some require a touch to the flower or a light breeze, but some don't need even a whisper. Others require pollen from another flower of the same species, and nature has created some ingenious methods to make this happen. These requirements will be detailed with each plant as it is discussed.

Wind-Pollinated Flowers

Wind-pollinated plants possess very fine grains of pollen that can be transferred from one flower to another on the very lightest breeze. Usually this type is released from long, dangling filaments that whip in the wind: for example, grasses, pussy willow-catkins and sweetcorn. In response, the stigma protrudes her stigmatic surfaces in order to catch the passing grains. Hay fever is cased by the presence of this type of pollen.

Many trees, shrubs and plants carry both male and female flowers, not always together, but near at hand. For instance, in sweetcorn the male flower is situated high on the plant and sheds its golden grains upon the female growing at a lower level; beech and the hazel do the same. The holly tree is either male or female, and needs the assistance of insects to ensure pollination. The female produces the lovely red berries containing the seed for future generations. The flowers are notable for their lack of pretty colours, adornments or even scents, and in the majority of cases there are no nectaries, either; instead there is a larger receptive stigma capable of holding on to any golden grains of pollen that alight on the sticky head. Gardeners often complain that their particular holly tree is not bearing any berries, when in fact what they have failed to realize is that theirs is a male plant and is busy pollinating the berries on the female tree next door.

Self-Pollinated Flowers

The self-pollinating method of reproduction is used by such plants as the sweet pea and the tomato. The stigma and the stamens lie in close proximity in the bud of the bloom, and are often pollinated before the flower even opens. To hybridize this type of plant, early intervention is required so

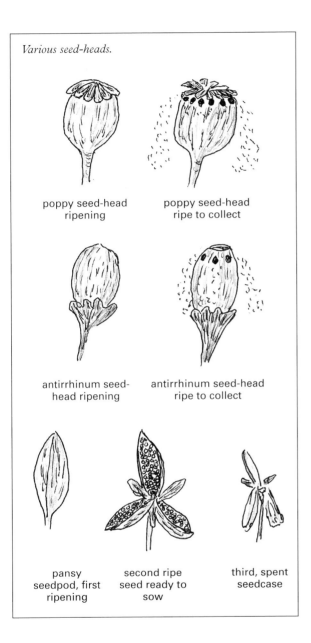

Various seed-heads.

poppy seed-head ripening

poppy seed-head ripe to collect

antirrhinum seed-head ripening

antirrhinum seed-head ripe to collect

pansy seedpod, first ripening

second ripe seed ready to sow

third, spent seedcase

are indeed listed. Each pollen grain carries an ancestral bank of genes ready to merge with the female stigma, which has a similar bank of genes, though its own variety. If the producing flowers come from the same family, then their individual genetic construction will be almost identical.

Pollen is the vital link in the reproductive process of the living plant. Some plants are self-pollinating and will be fertilized after pollination by their own

Seedling pinks under trial.

the pollinating procedure may be successfully manipulated. If it receives the attention of bees or insects, pollination is more assured. Self-pollination stabilizes genetic reliability, which is why seed can be saved from this type of plant in order to continue an identical line, with very little variation from plant to plant.

Birds may have a role to play, too: for instance, birds help the crocus to shed its pollen. Many people find it hard to forgive birds their habit of pecking the petals, but in fact this ensures a shaking, enough to dust the pollen onto the crocus's vital parts at a time when insects are perhaps weatherbound.

Many plants have a built-in self-incompatibility, a method that resists self-pollination, thus ensuring outbreeding, and offspring with more variability than the self-pollinating types. Some plants achieve this self-incompatibility because of the way the flower functions. The dianthus group is an example, where the stamens and the pollen on the plant become ripe, and the grains are scattered, before the arrival of the stigma, which comes later and so has to wait for pollen from another flower.

The delphinium is another interesting plant, and exemplifies nature's way to get an outcross, even if from its own plant. Bees will always visit the lower florets of a spike first, these having a high nectar supply. On the lower florets the stamens have probably gone past their best, but significantly the nectar flowers are at their best when the stigma is ripe. The bee searches though the flowers from the bottom to the top, so on leaving it takes the ripe pollen from the upper florets; so when it alights on the lower florets on a spike, pollen from another plant would be present on the insect, thus supplying the needs of the lower, prime stigma.

Differently coloured flowers on the same stem. The top one is split through the centre.

Insect-Pollinated Plants

These plants are generally colourful, attractive to the eye, and often scented, and many supply a meal of sweet nectar thus ensuring the attention of plenty of hungry insects. But in helping themselves to a free snack, the insects play an important part in transferring pollen from one flower to another or, as is sometimes the case, in ensuring that pollen is applied in profusion to the same flower, guarantee of a perfect pollination. Little do they realize that they are actually working for a living, and a full stomach means they are happy to call again.

FERTILIZATION

Once perfect pollination has taken place, the process of fertilization is activated when the pollen grains feed on the stigma juices and microscopic tubes grow down the style to fertilize the ovules, so creating the seed. Even after a perfect application of pollen there is sometimes no guarantee of success,

mainly because the stigma has to be in a receptive condition and ripe before the pollen tubes can proceed to the ovary.

If all is well, the swelling of the seedpod soon becomes evident. The next step is to keep a watchful eye on the ripening process, and gather the seed at the appropriate time.

PARENT SELECTION

Having decided on the species of plant best suited for genetic manipulation, the first step is to select the finest parents possible. Good parents that are sound in all respects must be the only choice, healthy and strong, and possessing the ideal qualities of the species selected.

Whilst studying the plants in the course of parental selection, many differences heretofore untoward and unnoticed will be apparent. Sometimes there are extreme differences that are indistinguishable at first sight, but on close scrutiny can be detected. Making a note of all the finer points as

Seedling pink, still only a number.

Another seedling pink, still only a number.

well as the deficiencies will help in arriving at the best overall assessment of the quality of the stock on hand, and this will prove the finest guide to the selection of future parents.

If any plant has an unfavourable defect for its type, discard its potentiality as a parent, because once such a defect is introduced into a breeding line, eradicating it is often difficult; avoiding setbacks inevitably helps progress.

Assessing stock can become an intriguing pastime, and certainly relevant to the essential need to discover the individual qualities on which to build. Thus, one plant may possess wonderful leaves in shape and size as compared to others in the stock, but less distinguishing flowers. Another perhaps shows off a most beautiful bloom in shape and colour, but has poor leaf formation. Bringing these plants together in the cross-breeding programme will, put simply, jumble up the genes, both dominant and recessive, and these will pair off to give a mixture of good and inferior

leaves in combination with wonderful blooms and inferior flowers. After nature has played her part it is likely that as well as plants with poor flowers and nondescript blooms, there are also wonderful flowers in combination with good leaf formation. This is put simply, and merely goes to show what can be achieved, although more promising results emerge from more intricate methods.

It is sound advice to visit flower shows with the intention of observing the finest plants of your chosen species, and consider purchasing some top quality varieties to form the basis of your breeding programme. It may take you years to reach the same standard as the plants in the show using your present stock; but start at a relatively high level using top quality bought plants, and you are already part way up the progress ladder. In horse racing, the very best purpose-bred stallion would be used to produce a Derby winner, and you must think along the same lines and start with the very best to achieve the results you want.

New seedling.

BELOW: *New seedling, new colour.*

OUTCROSSING AND INBREEDING

Plants are naturally constructed in two ways, some for the inbred (self-fertilizing) adaptation, and others for the outcross (cross-fertilization) method. Examples of the inbred types are all the pea family, including broom, garden peas and sweet peas; these are self-pollinated because the stamens lie in close proximity to the stigma in the flower bud, and both are ripe before the bud opens, meaning that fertilization is under way before the flower is fully open. This is nature's way of inbreeding, and can be of great assistance to the plant breeder who wants to marry this approach to a particular programme. There are many other ways of inbreeding, but these will be discussed in more detail when applied to a particular operation.

The dianthus family's breeding technique is another of nature's ingenious ways, in this instance

New seedlings.

to encourage outcrossing. As the flower opens, the stamens grow out from its centre; when they have reached full length, they open, to offer their pollen to any inquisitive insect.

They also open two at a time, thus offering the pollen over a longer period. Then, as they come to the end of their spell as pollen supplier, the stigma start growing, slowly getting longer until they protrude way out above the petals, until finally the two stigma horns begin to curl at the ends. This is when the plant is pollinated by an insect bearing the pollen from another flower, thereby completing another of nature's wonderful ways of manipulating results.

Taking a plant from an inbred progeny, the genetic constitution will be as a block of genes with limited variability, building in to each generation the same supply of genetic material, and thereby creating a similarity among the offspring. However, if a new plant of the same species but from a completely different family group were crossed with the inbred plant, then the block of genes from each plant would be combined, and a very mixed family of seedlings would result, usually with a great percentage of inferior stock.

By way of allegory, replace the seedlings with children, and the genes with clothes. Now for every child place a number of different coloured clothes in a container, enough for everyone to wear. Next the children are blindfolded, and asked to dress in the clothes they pick out at random – and it is highly unlikely that any would have anything matching; and this is the conclusion we must draw when aiming for perfection. Some combinations are quite fascinating, and are acceptable as something new; and in reality these are the ones we keep an eye out for. The same applies if, using the same hypothesis, we limit the number of colours: this would increase the chances of a closer match, as applies to our seedlings with a limited number of genes. It is now possible to accept the fact that nothing is perfection, and we can at least attempt to prove this theory wrong.

Back to genetics, it can now be realized that after an outcross has been made in order to breed new genes into the family, selection isolates the best of the seedlings, which hopefully carry the quality genes. The better seedlings, those which appear to be enriched with the ideal commodities, are then either back-crossed to the best parent, crossed with an equally quality sister seedling, or left to self-cross. This does not add any more genes to the bank, but utilizes the better ones already present in the selected seedlings. Further back-crossing may be required, together with selection, in order to eliminate unwanted traits, leaving the possibility of combining the genetic make-up to supply perfection.

In the preferred types for inbreeding, the vigour is maintained even if the inbreeding process has continued for many years; the outbreeders, on the other hand, would suffer in vitality and quality if used in an inbreeding capacity over a long period.

Many plants are self-incompatible, although some are more variable than others, as already explained in the dianthus pollinating process. Thus, although the dianthus can be pollinated by its own pollen, the pollen has to come from a different flower, even if this is another, younger flower on the same plant. Another such example of this process is the petunia, which has to receive pollen from another flower, as each flower is a preferred outbreeder.

Nature has many methods of creating incompatibility in the types of flowers intended for natural cross-pollination. The mechanics applied to some are most ingenious, but all have the simplicity of nature in the finest form: take as an example the flowers of the primula species, a simple primrose or polyanthus. Two types of flower will be found, the pin-head and the thrum-head. The former shows the stigma high in the flower centre, with stamens down at the base of the flower. The latter has the reverse, showing a lovely, prettier bloom, parading the golden fluffy stamens at the uppermost part, with the stigma on a short style at the base of the flower tube.

Both these types serve the purpose of ensuring a cross is made between the two, with the assurance that pollen may fall onto the stigma to provide some seed, should the weather be unfavourable and prevent the insects from assisting with pollination so early in the year. In most cases the size of the pollen grains vary, showing that pollen grains from the thrum are too large for its own stigma, which requires the smaller-grained pollen of the

Another variety of new seedling.

pin-head plant, and *vice versa*. More seed is produced by the pin-head plant, hence the prominence of the stigma. The thrum-head, on the other hand, makes for a better pollen plant whilst the pin-head is an ideal seed bearer.

Another plant using an incompatibility technique is the pansy or viola; this is completely different from the primula species method, but just as effective. In the pansy flower the stigma protrudes from the flower with a lip at the very tip. Below this the five stamens surround the waist of the stigma tube, rather like a belt: these contain the pollen. As the bee probes into the flower to collect the nectar, pollen rubs off the body of the bee into the stigma cup, so performing the cross-pollination as nature intended. As the bee reverses from the flower, more pollen is collected onto its body; but as it passes out past the stigma, its body pushes the lip closed over the mouth of the stigma, thus preventing self-pollination. Other intricate methods are used, but all these will be discussed in the relevant chapters on the plants concerned.

FLOWERS

African Violets

SIMPLICITY GUIDE

Measure of difficulty	Crossing stage	Flower to seed	Seed germination	Seedling stage
FAIRLY EASY	FAIRLY EASY	EASY	EASY	CARE REQUIRED

SITES FOR BEST RESULTS Warm, light position in north-facing window is ideal, not full sun.
SPECIAL NOTES The seed is tiny; keep sterile conditions when handling or sowing the seed.

The African violet is a very well known and extreme-ly popular plant, and is recorded as having been found just over one hundred years ago: this was apparently in 1890 by Baron Walter von Saint Paul, in the wilds of East Africa – Tanzania and Kenya – hence its official name of 'Saint Paulia'. Seeds were sent to Europe and plants were first seen at horti-cultural shows in 1893, although the type was unknown in America until the 1920s.

The African violet makes a lovely windowsill plant; it flourishes in the warmth of the home and is easy to grow, making it the perfect subject to try out the fundamentals of creating a new flower – even with one plant, seed can be obtained by pollinating the plant with its own pollen. However, the plant cannot easily accomplish this without assistance from the plant breeder. Nevertheless, the method of using one plant to supply the seed can often provide excellent plants – though using pollen from anoth-er plant, outcrossing, is still the most plausible way to achieve the new varieties we aim to find.

Select a healthy specimen, one that is already in bloom will give an early start. Study the flower closely to examine the vital organs at the centre of the bloom. The illustrations on page 17 will show two pollen sacs in the flower centre; these are quite firm and dry to the touch. Just above them is the stigma (the pin-head) held up by the style, and at the base can be seen the ovary or seed container.

The best time to cross this plant is when the petals either droop or fall; the pollen is ripe at this stage, and the stigma may be. Once the petals, plus the pollen

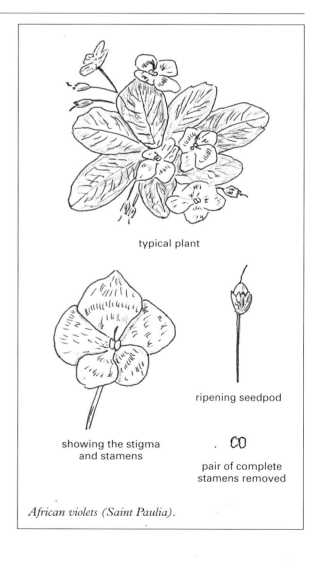

typical plant

showing the stigma and stamens

ripening seedpod

pair of complete stamens removed

African violets (Saint Paulia).

Good flowers with good pollen sacs.

BELOW: *The yellow pollen and long stigma are easily seen.*

BELOW RIGHT: *The petals and pollen sacs have dropped leaving the stigma ready to be pollinated.*

sacs, have dropped, the stigma is left erect and exposed, and ready to be pollinated, its tip now sticky in readiness to hold on to any pollen touching it.

The pollen sacs can be opened by splitting with a pin, or the end nipped off to expose the golden grains. Touch the pin-head stigma very gently with the pollen, and examine with the magnifying glass to be certain that the pollen has adhered; this completes the first part of the operation. Keep the sacs dry, and touch with the pollen the following day to be sure of a take.

When the pollen sacs drop from the plant they often never open, which is why the pin method is applied. If pollen is ripe on the plant before the stigma is sticky on the second plant, which in this case would be the seed parent, it is necessary to keep the pollen sacs in a dry state until the stigma is in a ripe condition for the pollen to adhere to it.

The seedpod will show signs of swelling even in a week or so, and as the pod develops, the stem will twist and turn in all directions; this period of ripening is rather a slow process, but other blooms will continue to flourish to keep the plant interesting whilst waiting for developments.

Once the full seedpod size is reached, there is a period when nothing seems to change, staying green for weeks until the brown, ripe conditions shows you have finally earned your precious seed. These are very fine, almost dust-like in constitution, and must be handled in sterilized conditions to prevent contamination from fungal or other diseases.

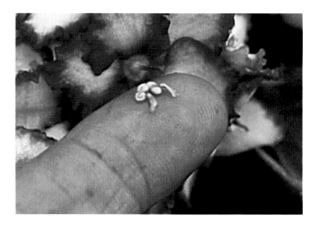

Pollen sacs removed.

Seed pod developing.

TO GROW THE SEED

It is best to sprinkle the seed onto clean kitchen paper, then dust it with a proprietary seed coating; this helps to prevent the dreaded damping off disease.

Use ericaceous compost, mixed with silver sand to give an open texture. Soak well with sterilized water: ideally boil some rainwater in a pan, then let it cool. Level off the surface, then sprinkle the coated seed onto the damp compost. Do not cover the seed with compost, but enclose the container in clingfilm or a plastic bag, placing it in a warm, light position away from the sun. The ideal seed temperature is between 18 and 20°C (65–70°F), and the plants to be grown at a temperature of no lower than 10°C (50°F).

African violets dislike lime, so if boiled soft rainwater can be used, the results will be greatly improved. The more seed that can be put down the better, as they are so tiny as to be hardly visible; as they germinate they form little plantlets, and obviously many seeds will give more plantlets so the surface will look lush and green; with only a few seeds they are almost impossible to see in the early stages.

As long as they don't dry out, the plants can be left in the containers until large enough to be handled and potted on individually. Keep the young plantlets moist and in a humid atmosphere if possible, and give a liquid feed every second watering. As the plants develop they can be fed until they reach full size, which could be around six months. On no account must they be overwatered, as this practice will lead to rotting at ground level.

The feed should be stopped at this point to encourage the formation of the first flowers, some eight to ten months after sowing the seed. Although this sounds a long time, it is also in fact the time taken for a leaf cutting to produce its first bloom.

At the first sign of flower buds on the plant, give a weak liquid potash fertilizer; this will mature the plant and encourage plenty of flowers. The opening of your very first flower is most exciting and a thrill that is repeated every time a new plant shows its potential: it is this that stimulates the hybridizer to aim for more exotic things.

The self-crossed plant will produce less variety of seedlings than the outcrossed plants, being a mixture of just one plant's genes in the first cross, as opposed to a combination of two sets of genes from the two plants in the second. However, it does not follow that any one of the seedlings is better than another: they all have the potential to be of star quality, especially if the parents are quality plants.

SELECTING

When all the seedlings are in bloom an assessment can be made and the quality plants selected, or the preferred ones according to choice. These can in turn be used to continue the breeding line, crossing the very best seedlings with each other, also the very best seedlings back to the best parent. Some extremely good results can be expected by self-crossing some of the better seedlings.

A keen eye is required at this point to scrutinize the young plants for any defects in quality, however small. Any plant showing any kind of failing is best not integrated into the breeding programme, because once a fault is introduced into a breeding line, it becomes very difficult to eradicate.

Seedlings of particular quality can be multiplied by taking leaf cuttings: these will produce a plant identical to the one from which it was taken.

SEEDLING CARE

It is important to water seedlings only with soft water: warmed rainwater is the ideal, although in some areas of the country the water from the mains is soft; in many others, however, it is very hard, and detrimental to African violets.

They respond favourably to warm, light conditions, but prefer a north-facing window away from hot sunshine, as this has a tendency to scorch the foliage. A sunny window protected by a net curtain would provide a good position for the plant, and if placed on a moist gravel base the extra humidity will be beneficial, especially if the growing position is protected from draughts.

MULTIPLYING THE STOCK

Once your favourite seedling is established, the means of producing many more of the same is simple enough – by leaf cutting. These can be started by taking a well-developed leaf cut from the plant, standing it in soft, sterilized water just 2.5cm (1in) deep, so that only the stem end is submerged; the water can be topped up if the need arises. Or, place the cutting into a rooting medium such as sand and peat or ericaceous potting compost. Select a healthy leaf, not too large, as smaller leaves take more quickly than larger ones. Don't go too far in this direction, however, as tiny leaves – as might be expected – produce tiny seedlings that take longer to catch up.

When the leaf is cut from the plant, also slit the stem end 13mm (½in) lengthways, then leave the cut surface to dry for a couple of hours before placing in the medium chosen. Dip the cutting into hormone powder containing fungicide, as this is an insurance against stem rot, and the extra slit in the stem will provide a bigger root growth area. A small glass container, similar to a pill container and with coloured glass, is perfect. A better rooting cluster will form in this type of container, also there will be less green algae to spoil the end result. If by any chance the end of the stem rots in the water, this can be cut away and the leaf replaced to try again, changing the water first. Don't forget to mark a label to name the leaf parent. Like the plants, place the leaf container in a light, warm position away from the sun.

POTTING ON

When the leaf cuttings have roots 6mm (¼in) long, they can be potted on into a mixture of sand and perlite or vermiculite to get them to develop a better root system. The new plantlets will be forming on the stem and also on the leaf; these will continue to flourish as the roots on the leaf develop and can be carefully removed and placed on a bed of vermiculite to continue to send down their own root systems when large enough to handle. Cover with clingfilm for a few days to assist the plantlets to establish. As the vermiculite contains no food, it will help the plantlets to dampen with weak liquid feed to assist development until they are ready for their final potting.

Aquilegias

SIMPLICITY GUIDE

Measure of difficulty	Crossing stage	Flower to seed	Seed germination	Seedling stage
EASY	EASY	EASY	EASY	EASY

SITES FOR BEST RESULTS Full sun or dappled shade. Will tolerate most soil conditions.
SPECIAL NOTES One of the best plants for beginners. Blooms in the early summer.

The aquilegia ranks among the prettiest of flowers, yet it has that inbuilt hardiness that helps it survive the cruellest of winters, belying its tender look. The range of types and the diversity typical of this plant place it in an enviable position, namely to be a selected candidate for the plant breeder. Once the crossing technique is mastered, intricate colour combinations are possible as well as all sorts of flower variations, many of which are beautiful; these vary according to the type of parent plants used.

This plant is native to the northern hemisphere and is found in many countries in that area. The most common of the species, *A. vulgaris*, is well known as 'Granny's Bonnets', and once introduced to a garden will seed each year all over the place. The more intricate types, on the other hand, are not so ardent, and all tend to be short-lived as perennials, but to compensate for this they will supply plenty of seed to replenish all losses.

There are many height variations to the species, from dwarf rockery types to the 1m (3ft) ones generally found in the cottage garden. The dwarf *A. Alpina* grows to 45cm (18in); it has lovely blue flowers and grows well in a rich, well drained soil. There is a smaller one, *A. jonesii*, that is quite uncommon but is ideal for an alpine house; it has small rosettes of leaves with blue flowers just popping above them. Then there is *A. longissima* that grows to 50cm (20in) with spurs of an extraordinary 10cm (4in) in length. There are many other varieties on the market all giving the potential of crossbreeding material.

Full flower; the stamens have to be removed before the pollen ripens.

All these species have beautiful leaves, adding to the graceful appearance of the plant and creating a wonderful backdrop to the delicate flowers; indeed, it can take a position anywhere in the garden.

All are clump forming, and the clumps can very often be split during the late autumn or early spring – although as mentioned earlier, they are short-lived and multiply by seeds.

For simplicity in crossing flowers, the aquilegia is second to none: the elegance of the flower, together with its undoubted hardiness, make it a foolproof candidate for the beginner as well as a wonderful subject for the specialist breeder. Impressive results may be gained from selective breeding with most of the aquilegia species. Select the proposed parents carefully: for instance, if you fancy the long-spurred types, then use the longest spurred plants you possess as the parents – and if good quality parents are not on hand, then the purchase of the appropriate type will save a disappointing result. Keep a critical eye on quality in every department: for instance, it may be found that the longer the spurs, the spindlier the stems become, and if a particular plant throws offspring with this unfavourable characteristic, discard it from your breeding programme. Some glorious colour combinations can be obtained in this way. For instance, excellent combinations can be achieved by crossing one bicolour with another, although not all the resulting seedlings will necessarily be bicolours. If, on the other hand, a combination of your favourite colours appears in the seedlings, then the procedure is to isolate this seedling and cross the flower with pollen from another flower on the same plant; although the aquilegia tends to be a preferred outcrossing plant, it will inbreed if pollen from another flower on the same plant is applied.

THE CROSS

When satisfied that the stock to be used as parents is up to standard, pot up the ones required for breeding so as to isolate them when in flower: when in full flower this will protect them from the honey bee, that will no doubt carry a different pollen from the one you want to use. Select a flower bud that is not yet open but on the verge of being so. Open the flower by either cutting the petals with small scissors or tearing them with fine tweezers to expose the inner parts. Gently remove

the stamens, but protect the stigmas – and check to make certain the stigmas are clean and free from any unwanted pollen; this is where the magnifying glass is essential.

This procedure is best performed in an isolated place, where the plant can be left until the pollen from the other flower is to be applied. The stigmas often have to be left for a day or two before they become ripe, ready for the pollen. To be more certain of the cross being the one you have administered you could cover the flower bud with a protective paper bag all through the operation, only removing it when the seedpod shows signs of development. When special individual plants are used, mark the

The type of bud used to emasculate.

Bud opened showing the stamens to be removed.

plant with a code number and apply the numbers to the seeds and the seedlings in case of back-crossing to the parent. Without some record to follow it is so easy to forget which plant the seedlings came from, which would be particularly disappointing when a colour combination is up to your requirements and a back-cross could fix it permanently.

It is most rare to find problems in this procedure, and plenty of seed can be expected.

THE SEED

Seed can be gathered as soon as it is ripe, and can be saved if preferred until the spring. It is a good idea to sow as soon as it is available, sowing in trays if many seedlings are wanted, but in pots if only a few are required. If sown straightaway, a good germination percentage will be acquired, plus the seedlings will have a good root system by the time winter arrives. The seedlings would then survive harsh conditions if planted outside: the leaves would wither away, but would emerge quite healthily in the spring. Alternatively it may be preferable not to put them to the test, but to grow them on in a cool greenhouse or in a cold frame. This way they

keep their leaves and make steady progress continually through to the spring, developing a good root system; a flying start is then guaranteed. Once hardened off they can be planted out in their flowering position and will be in bloom long before the ones planted outside in the autumn; this is definitely an advantage when wishing to procure a back-cross to a preferred parent, when you will have the seed early enough to take advantage of the late summer weather.

ABOVE: *Stamens removed leaving the stigma to be pollinated.*

Seed pods developing.

Seedlings pricked out into seed trays, if grown this way.

SEEDLING TESTING

If the seed is sown in a trial bed in the late summer the seedlings will flower later in the following season, usually after the parent plants are over; they can then be assessed on their own qualities. This is an ideal way to produce lots of plants, which can be sorted out as to their merits any time during the growing season; however, it is too late to make this season's back-cross, so losing a full year in the breeding programme.

Close examination of the seedlings in bloom will show evidence of any quality required to proceed to perfection: because most plants today are hybrids, any combination of colours will arise from the F1 – but if a seedling possesses a colour combination conducive to the programme, this flower can be self-crossed with another flower on the same plant. This will still harvest a mixed bag of seedlings, but it will also bring out some that will be comparable to the parents, and probably ideal to the next stage. These seedlings will be the F2 generation and should be selected and self-crossed again, which should supply many more of the type and colour of your selected ideal. By continuing this selfing procedure a family of plants looking very much alike will be on offer. This method will also fix the type

preferred; for instance, if the trait for long spurs was the intention, then only the longest spurred plants should be selected and crossed.

If a method of open ground sowing was undertaken to improve the stock, then seed should be saved from the plants showing the nearest to your favourite choice, and each season only gather seed from the plants showing the traits required. The improvement will continue each season until you will have a strain of plants as ideal to your choice as can be gained.

A WORD OF WARNING

One point of warning, which needs careful attention: in selfing as suggested with a preferred outbreeder (as this plant is), there can be a natural depression in the plants, leading to deterioration; in particular this can happen if selfing is prolonged. If two identical lines are used for the same combination, they can be crossed over at a later time when this outcross will return the hybrid vigour.

This is a beautiful plant to grow, and will serve well to adorn any position wherever planted. It is rather prone to aphid attack, but this is quite easy to eradicate; a clean plant is a healthy one.

Begonias

Measure of difficulty	Crossing stage	Flower to seed	Seed germination	Seedling stage
DIFFICULT	FAIRLY EASY	EASY	EXPERIENCED ONLY	FAIRLY EASY

SITES FOR BEST RESULTS Sunny, well drained site: hanging baskets, tubs, window boxes, borders.

SPECIAL NOTES The seeds are very tiny and require sterile procedure as suggested in the following chapter.

Any flower show throughout the country exhibiting the begonia, especially the large-flowered kind, always attracts the crowds because of the fascination for the wonderful colour variations now available. Most people look in wonder at the size and magnificent exotic colour range, almost in disbelief that a flower could exhibit such qualities.

Although this section is undoubtedly the favourite one, there are many species of begonia that can contribute to the popularity of the plant. The semperflorens are grown in abundance and give a marvellous show wherever they are planted, continuing until the first frost cuts them down. Many offices and homes are adorned with the cane-stemmed variety such as *B. lucerne* or the foliage variety *B. rex*. And there are the tuberous varieties of multifloras and cascades, all beautiful plants in their own right, and every one offering the possibility of a cross-pollination to produce something completely new with the assistance of the hybridist.

Millions of begonias of every variety are grown throughout the world, and the popularity of this plant has been brought about by the introduction of the many species gathered by the travellers. Nurserymen sent out researchers to find and bring back all kinds of plants to boost their sale of exotic species.

During the 1860s Messrs James Veitch introduced varieties brought to this country from South America, all of them single varieties. But it wasn't long before hybridists were creating new hybrids possessing fascinating flower and leaf colour combinations. Up to the present day only a very few species have been used in the expansion of the varieties, with many neglected types almost cast aside as being inferior to the programme – indeed many could be lost for ever as interest concentrates on the few to the detriment of the majority.

VARIETY SELECTION

There are many choices when deciding which variety to manipulate, and concentrating on one line is sound advice, and one that could well lead to success. And achieving results at the first attempt means certain addiction to a lifetime of crossbreeding.

The large-flowered types of *B. tuber* hybrids are amongst the more popular that are crossbred today, many new varieties being added each year, the fascinating selection of a vast range of colours being combined with frilled petals, picotee versions, single, semi-double and double blooms. The cascade types are ideal for hanging baskets and have been developed by the plant breeder to possess larger flowered, stronger stemmed pendulas, both qualities necessary to support the blooms in the face of strong winds sometimes encountered in a hanging basket.

The *B. semperflorens* are grown by seed merchants in vast numbers to cope with the demand for this bedding variety. The compactness and colour range, as well as the floriferous display of this plant, means that nurserymen must grow as many as possible so as to meet the demand of the bedding schemes used throughout the country.

Every garden centre and nursery, even supermarkets, stock this popular plant to satisfy the needs of the public.

Visit a flower show with the begonia listed in its schedule and you will be amazed at the quality of the exhibits. Many newcomers to the growing of the begonia were initially inspired by the sight of such magnificent exhibits.

BREEDING YOUR OWN

If you are a beginner to the crossbreeding of this species, whichever variety is selected to be attempted, it is advisable only to cross like with like to start with. Experiment with the more sophisticated crosses when early success has been achieved, and confidence is at its premium.

On examining a begonia's blooms it will be noticed that there are two types of flower on the same plant: the female flower is recognized by the winged seedpod (ovary) below the usually single flower. The male flower is more likely to be the bigger and more spectacular bloom, and this is the pollen carrier with only a plain stem behind the flower.

To administer the cross, all that is required is to collect ripe pollen from the male stamens, placing it onto the ripe stigma of the female flower. The pollen on the male bloom is ready when it takes on a fluffed up appearance, and easily adheres to the finger tips or a small artist's brush. At this stage it can be gently stroked onto the flower possessing a ripe stigma – this is recognized by the glossy, sticky solution to be seen at the stigma tips, when the pollen will readily adhere and is easily seen by the naked eye. The next step will be to mark the plants with the parentage details and dates.

Sometimes the selected male flower, and especially of the large-flowered types, will be reluctant to produce pollen. There is so much emphasis on producing an abundance of petals, that the stamens take on the roll of extra petals to the detriment of pollen production.

Sometimes a male flower is in a ripe condition and the pollen ready, but the selected female flower is still not in a receptive condition to receive it: this impasse can be overcome by placing the pollen in a glass jar and keeping it in a refrigerator until required.

If however, the female flower is receptive and the pollen ripe, then pollination may be completed.

If there is little or no pollen on the male flower you want to use, wait until the bloom is beginning to fade; just before it is obviously collapsing, look into the centre and at this time there is usually enough pollen to administer the cross. In a few days the female flower will fade and die, leaving the seedpod beneath to swell. From this time on, carefully monitor the development of the seedpod: in a few weeks' time the stem will start to dry, indicating that no more nourishment is being administered to the seedpod, and at this point it may be removed.

The problem of the double flowers not producing enough pollen can sometimes be overcome by taking a cutting, or a small piece of tuber with an eye later in the season. These will develop smaller plants which in turn will throw out single flowers which will produce the needed pollen from that variety.

THE SEED

After the removal of the dried seedpod, place on a large white sheet of paper on a tray. Place in a dry area where the seed case will dry and split open. Usually the seed stays nearby on the paper, not popping off like pansy seed would. When dry completely, the rest of the contents can be shaken from the dried casing. The seed is minute in size, but many hundreds can be gathered in the hope of something special. The seed can be kept until early sowing next season; fold them in tissue paper, and place them in a glass jar in a cold position, even in the refrigerator, though not the freezer. This will keep them in the peak of vitality ready for a flying start when sown.

SOWING

Take extra care when sowing very small seed like the begonia – the results will prove worthwhile. Mix three parts good quality seed compost with one part sharp sand and fill the pot, pan or box, depending on the quantity of seed to be sown; this gives excellent drainage. Pour boiling water over the compost in the pot to sterilize both pot and soil, then leave to cool and drain. Level the surface and sprinkle the seed finely. Do not cover the seed with compost, as light is required for germination. Spray the seed with cooled, boiled water mixed with fungicide, using a very fine spray; this is to protect the seed from any contamination existing on the seed from the store process or chaff from the seedpod. Cover the top of the pot with clingfilm tied with an elastic band or cord around the rim, and place in a propagator maintained at 18–20°C (65–70°F).

GERMINATION

At any time from ten days on, the first seedlings should be appearing. Give plenty of light, which is essential at this stage, though not in bright sunshine; the clingfilm can be left on for a few days until the seedlings take on a more robust stature. You can leave the film on for a few days with confidence because you know the seed is protected by the fungicide sprayed on the seed and compost before you covered it. When the clingfilm is removed, do not subject the tender seedlings to too big a temperature change, as they are very vulnerable at this time. As regards watering, never let the surface dry out; and when the next watering is due, depending on the conditions, take care to spray with tepid fungicide water, not cold, or the chill will cause the seedlings to collapse.

In around a month's time the little plants will be ready to be moved to mini pots with fresh compost, and the earlier the moves the better they seem to grow; an excellent indication of progress is when the first true leaves appear. Once transplanted, the ideal conditions are to grow in a warm environment, still at the above temperature; do not water or spray from the top, however, because the true leaves need to be dry – keep just the soil moist.

FINAL POSITION

If only a few plants are grown and the intention is to keep them inside, then keep them in the same ideal conditions, moving them on to larger pots as required until flowering time in the greenhouse. If,

on the other hand, planting out is the aim, then harden off the plants in a cold frame before attempting to plant outdoors.

Plants for outside bedding can be put in place after the hardening off period is complete and all fear of frost has passed. Plant them preferably in a spot sheltered from the hot midday sun and in particular strong winds, which could well snap the stem of your large prize bloom.

Grow on until quality and attributes can be assessed, and those candidates worthy of the next stage in the production programme selected.

ASSESSMENT TIME

By midsummer the seedlings will be showing their true characteristics, whether quality attributes or undesired frailties handed down through the genetic capabilities of their parents. Of course, we are hoping for an abundance of the qualities and very few of the weaknesses – but Mother Nature has the deciding toss of the coin in this respect. Note all the good qualities, and check each plant for those characteristics that tempted you to choose the parents in the first place: if these finer points are visible in the new seedling, then the first stage of the programme has been successfully achieved. The next step is to study all the seedling assessments, when it should become apparent as to which pairings of seedlings should now be used for crossing in order to cement the ideal characteristics, placing these into a dominant genetic necessity to carry to the next generation.

In the autumn, when the plants begin to die back, the tubers can be cleaned and stored in a frost-free area. In the case of the semperflorens, seed is the usual way to reproduce plants for the following season, when you can look forward to the same thrill of checking out the qualities of the seedlings. Most growers of these garden favourites throw away the plants at the onset of winter, not realizing that these too can be kept and planted in the spring. I once grew some semperflorens in the gravel drive close to the house, where they gave a wonderful show. When the frost finally cut them down to ground level, I left them in the gravel to overwinter. The winter was not too severe, and in the spring every single one of those plants came up and gave a better show than the previous year.

Watering and feeding the plants as they show through the surface will save expense and you will find they are of top quality.

Never lose sight of the fact that just as good qualities can be secured, so can unfavourable traits, and any seedlings showing signs of any sort of weakness must be discarded. The only way to success is by allowing only the improvements to the ideal plant to be perpetuated, and culling of the lesser quality seedlings is a must.

All classes of the begonia family can be accommodated in this same breeding method, and as experience is gained, more optimistic crosses can be attempted.

Chrysanthemums

SIMPLICITY GUIDE

Measure of difficulty	Crossing stage	Flower to seed	Seed germination	Seedling stage
FAIRLY DIFFICULT	DIFFICULT	FAIRLY EASY	EASY	EASY

SITES FOR BEST RESULTS Sunny, open position is best; will tolerate most soils.
SPECIAL NOTES Flowers later in the summer unless greenhouse-grown. Very tricky at the crossing stage, but from there on, it is easy.

Although the chrysanthemum is the emblem of Japan, it was in fact first cultivated in China, and was mentioned by Confucius in 500BC. It did not grace the Japanese mainland until over a hundred years later, but by then had travelled via Korea. This was the start of the type later known as the 'Japanese varieties', which came about by the Chinese plant cross-breeding with the wild Japanese native species; after a process of selection, these were introduced during the festivals that were very popular around AD900. It is interesting that the highest award that could then be given to a member of the public for services to the country was the Order of the Chrysanthemum.

The earliest recorded plant to be cultivated in England was in the mid-eighteenth century, and the first to arrive at Kew Gardens was in about 1795; this plant was called 'Old Purple' and is probably in the RHS libraries. Once this plant,

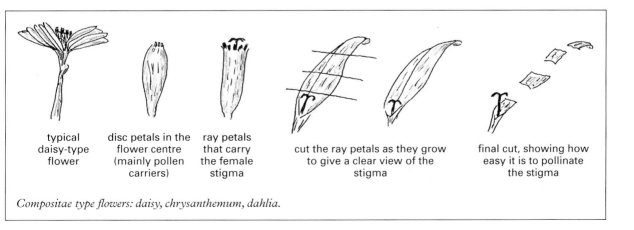

| typical daisy-type flower | disc petals in the flower centre (mainly pollen carriers) | ray petals that carry the female stigma | cut the ray petals as they grow to give a clear view of the stigma | final cut, showing how easy it is to pollinate the stigma |

Compositae type flowers: daisy, chrysanthemum, dahlia.

together with others from abroad, became established, it soon became so popular that shows were arranged in England, and this led to the idea of forming a society. At Stoke Newington in 1846 enthusiasts formed the National Chrysanthemum Society, and it is still one of the finest in the country.

The varieties to be seen at that time were far removed from the varieties on display today, but the members of that period are to be praised for laying such firm foundations, and those that followed for the advancement of this wonderful flower. The growers of chrysanthemums have always been amongst the most dedicated perfectionists, and are to be congratulated for producing the wonderful flowers we see on the show bench today. Anyone taking a first prize at a chrysanthemum show is indeed an enthusiastic gardener, and to win in any of the classes is an achievement. There is plenty of literature to guide the newcomer along the path to success, but none gives a shortcut to perfection: this takes time, thought and plenty of effort. Here we

intend to produce some new varieties, a task that will need true dedication in order to produce the quality shown on the show bench. Only good quality plants have a chance to score a first, and good quality seedlings can only come from top class stock, which is why the finest parents are required to start a breeding programme.

Those who are beginners to the skill of hybridizing the chrysanthemum would be advised to start with the single or semi-double types to get the feel of the petal arrangements, and gain an understanding of the basic procedure; this will give them a better chance of success. As mentioned before, it is a useful practice to strip a flower, petal by petal, as this will give valuable guidance to the best approach.

THE TASK

The chrysanthemum is assuredly more difficult to crossbreed than any of the other flowers referred to

here – once you know the method it does become easier. On inspection, the flower of the chrysanthemum looks a mass of petals, and newcomers to crossbreeding usually give up their attempt to try this flower. It is in fact a *compositae*, which means that it is made up of many florets, as a dandelion or a daisy: thus if you examine the bloom more closely by stripping the petals off, you will see that these are the florets, each a flower in its own right. Starting at the outside, you will notice that the outer florets contain the stigma, which will be the female in our cross and are called ray florets. Towards the centre of the bloom are the disc florets, which carry stamens and the pollen required.

The time to start the breeding programme is from the point of selecting and potting the cuttings of the varieties intended to take the role of parents; these miniature parents-to-be will live a different life from the ones destined for the show bench. Whereas the show plants will be tended with loving care to produce luscious, healthy flowers and foliage, the breeding pair will be planted in plain soil and grown on without extra food and only the minimum of water. The idea is to produce a smaller plant that will give a supply of poor flowers, many with fewer petals or florets, but hopefully with a better supply of pollen. Many plants used in exhibition, and not only chrysanthemums, are treated to the finest foods, and raised under ideal conditions so that they produce the large, high quality blooms we see on the show bench. All of these will make elaborate double flowers, using the stamens to develop more petals at the expense of the reproduction organs.

The parent plants can be grown on as suggested until they mature. No bud stopping is required, as all the flowers can be used; this is because many will come as single or semi-double, thus making pollinating much easier – besides which pollen should be more plentiful. Up to the point of showing colour, the plants can be grown outside; but then they should be placed in the greenhouse or on the windowsill to isolate them from pollen-bearing insects. As the buds expand and the flowers open, it will be noticed that the outer (ray) florets contain the stigma deep down in the floret.

If the petal part of the floret is cut off just above the stigma, then as the flower fully develops the stigma will grow above the cut floret, thus making it much easier to apply pollen.

Cutting the petals will take several days, a few at a time as the stigmas expand and ripen, and so on as more florets develop; and so the pollinating process will continue until the required crosses have been made. If this can be done away from insect interference, then there is no need to cut away the disc florets in the centre of the bloom to prevent self-pollination.

The above method is used to deal with the intended seed-bearing parent, but to get the pollen required, the other parent plant can be left to flower as above until the centre disc florets produce the necessary pollen – though this may not appear until the flower is on the wane. The poor flowers produced by this method in fact create the ideal conditions for cross-pollination.

This same principle can be applied with flowers cut from the plants that are grown outdoors. If taken with a long stem, placed in a deep vase and the water changed fairly often, the whole process can be completed on a windowsill; just cut the base of the stem occasionally to keep it fresh, and good results will be achieved.

After all the required crosses are complete and the labels safely in place, the stems can be left, as there is little to be done except keep watch on proceedings until the head is completely dry and almost falling apart. The seed will take six to eight weeks to ripen, but no attempt should be made to collect it until the head is fully dried. Then place the dried head either onto a tray or into a paper bag to complete the ripening process, where the seed can be separated from the rubbish.

SEED SOWING

Early February is an ideal time to sow the seed; if the intention is to grow many plants then seed trays are the most convenient, but if only a few seeds are sown then pots are best. Use a good seed compost, then water this well before placing the seed on the surface; then cover lightly with vermiculite or a light dressing of compost. At this point it is advisable to spray with a fungicide in case any seed has been contaminated in storage: this procedure will give a flying start to your seedlings. Place in the labels, then cover the boxes with glass, and put clingfilm over the pots, holding it fast with an elastic band; this will retain the moisture long enough for germination if the ambient temperature is maintained at 16°C (60°F).

As soon as the seedlings show their first leaves they must be placed in a position where they get plenty of light in order to grow on to be as stocky as possible. A leggy seedling never really recovers to display its highest potential, and after all the trouble it has taken to get this far it would be a shame to lose perfection at this stage. The potting on from this stage can be the same method as taken for developing the finest show plants. With exhibition-type care we can look forward to the first exhibition blooms from the seedlings; no one else will have a seedling the same as yours and the first time you glimpse the true quality of your very own plants is really exciting.

It is advisable to breed first with the early varieties that should flower before the end of September in the open ground; also keep the crosses to the confines of the types, such as reflex to reflex, incurve to incurve and singles the same. If you experience no problems, a more adventurous approach might be tried. Do not be surprised at the colours produced in the seedlings, because whatever the parents' colour, it does not follow that the seedlings will be of the same hue. There could be a real mixture, depending on the genes inherent to each parent; as with all plants growing today, they have experienced innumerable cross-pollinations by both man and the insect worlds, so the results could be legion. I have found that crossing two pale colours tends to produce poor specimens; but pale colours bred from a strong colour to a pale one have a better quality and more substance. There are naturally exceptions, and as long as only first quality plants are used as parents, then the chances of success are that much greater.

Clematis

SIMPLICITY GUIDE

Measure of difficulty	Crossing stage	Flower to seed	Seed germination	Seedling stage
CAN BE TRICKY	TRICKY	EASY	DIFFICULT	FAIRLY EASY

SITES FOR BEST RESULTS The plant is very tolerant and can grow almost anywhere. Likes a sunny site and something to climb up or cling to.

SPECIAL NOTES This is a very rewarding plant and if the methods are followed to the letter, brilliant flowers are sure to excite the grower.

This plant has forged ahead in popularity in recent years, mainly because of the wonderful variety of colour and the diversity of the flower. This puts the plant species in a very prominent position, where it might be taken over by the plant breeder of today to get the most elegant crossbred hybrids in the not-too-distant future. It is an excellent opportunity for the plant breeder to take advantage of the abundance of material, which he will use to blend and construct fantastic new plants.

It is only in the last couple of centuries that we have been blessed with large-flowered varieties; before then, only small-flowered species were to be found. The plant's rise to stardom has been through the introduction of large flowers, which in turn has gone hand in hand with the introduction of many new varieties. Furthermore, during the nineteenth century, the mania for possessing new species of all plants meant that thousands of various types from all corners of the globe were introduced. In the case of the clematis, species from the Continent, Asia, the Americas, China and Japan were soon to find a home in the gardens of stately homes all over England.

It was inevitable that some newer and more spectacular variations would be created from cross-breeding with the imports, but these were nothing compared to the promise of the quality of the ones just waiting to be released by the modern-day hybridist: there is a vast range of varieties he can select and manipulate in creating the type of new seedlings envisaged. And not just the types or the colours, but there are hundreds of species and literally thousands of varieties, from the small-flowered early spring arrivals through to the more flamboyant, luxurious blooms of the large-flowered, and then continuing into the late autumn.

Deciding which type of flower to explore for your future creation is a formidable task, but having done so it is advisable to cross similar types until experience is gained like this; there is more guarantee of success. Nothing is more harmful than to fail on the first attempt. Having studied various catalogues or enjoyed visits to specialist nurseries to see at first hand the varieties most suited to your adaptations, a start can be made from potted plants you have bought in, or indeed from ones already established in the garden.

HYBRIDIZING

The first step is to select the two varieties that are intended to be the parents. Choose a flower bud that is on the point of opening. Take off the sepals with a pair of tweezers, or even cut them off with a small pair of scissors, being constantly careful not to damage the internal organs of the bud. Take off the stamens, which at this stage should still be too immature to release pollen, leaving the stigma

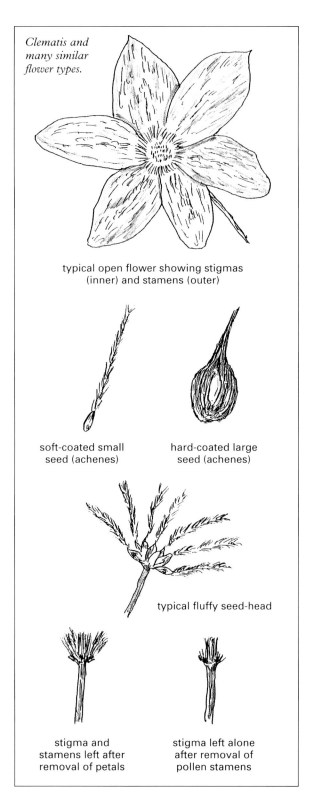

Clematis and many similar flower types.

typical open flower showing stigmas
(inner) and stamens (outer)

soft-coated small
seed (achenes)

hard-coated large
seed (achenes)

typical fluffy seed-head

stigma and
stamens left after
removal of petals

stigma left alone
after removal of
pollen stamens

'Nelly Moser'.

Both stigma and stamens are unripe at this stage.

intact. At this early stage the stigmas are also too immature to receive pollen, so must be left for a couple of days to ripen: they are ready when they become sticky at the ends with a viscous liquid. During the period before ripening it is wise to cover the bud with a paper bag to prevent stray pollen spoiling the cross.

ABOVE: *Flower showing stigma and stamens.*

LEFT: *Ideal bud to emasculate ready for pollination.*

When it is time to apply the pollen from the selected male plant, take a fully opened flower that has an abundance of pollen and touch the sticky stigmas with a dusting from the flower head. A small artist's brush can be used to transport the pollen from the stamens of one flower to the stigma of the other. Cover the bud once again to keep this operation safe, opening it again only to give a second application of pollen to be more certain of the cross. After a week the bag can be removed to allow the seed cluster to mature in the natural way. Label the cross with the parentage for future reference.

During the following weeks of maturity, the cluster will turn from dark green to brown when the stem, complete with the seed, can be stood in water until the seed is ready to part from the holder. Dry off completely for a few days on the windowsill. Sometimes certain varieties are a long time ripening their seed, and could go well into the winter before the ripening process is complete; these are mainly the late varieties. Naturally the earlier these varieties are crossed, the better the chances of ripening.

If it is intended to cross two varieties that flower at different times of the year, it is possible to save the pollen from the early flowering plant. Collect it

Stamens removed ready to be crossed.

when ripe on a warm dry day, place it in a small, airtight plastic container, and put it in the refrigerator until the other, later plant is in bloom.

SEED SOWING

The clematis seed cluster consists of many achenes or individual seed capsules with feathery tails, and although some species are completely different from others, the same principles apply. First and foremost, the harder the seed husk, the longer the seed will take to germinate. Some with small seeds will germinate within a few days, while others can take anything up to two years, depending on conditions at the time. The majority of the large-flowered types have larger seed, which can be tempted to germinate by the stratification process: this requires sowing the seed as soon as it is ripe into a very open-type compost, incorporating grit to allow for free drainage and air flow. Give the seed a light covering of grit; water well, then cover with clingfilm to retain moisture.

Place in a cold frame to endure the cold weather, which assists in breaking down the hard coating on the seed, also in removing any inhibitors present, to prepare for germination. Leave until the spring. It is a good idea to cover the pots with a piece of slate or wood to keep them dark to discourage early germination, in which case they must be frequently checked. When spring arrives the pots can be placed in the greenhouse to germinate. When the seedlings show, remove the covers to allow in the maximum amount of light possible; however, avoid direct sunshine as this can easily scorch the young seedlings.

POTTING ON

As the seedlings reach their two-leaf stage, remove them from the pots onto the greenhouse bench. Remove the whole soil-ball, and gently tease the tiny seedlings free without damaging the tender roots. Pot on into individual pots and then water, before placing them back into the position they were in, whether it was in the propagator or the greenhouse staging. After a few days of recuperation they can be grown on in the normal way, and hardened off ready for outside planting in the spring.

PLANTING OUT

When the time comes to plant out the new seedlings, it is wise to plant them in a nursery row to evaluate their potential properties before selecting a final planting position. These are new seedlings of unknown qualities, and a full assessment as to their hidden characteristics is advisable before a place on the floral stage can be permitted. All your own seedlings will have a special place in your heart as potential winners, but realistically we must cull the ones that fall short when compared to the quality of either of the two parents.

Selection is made as the young plants mature to the flowering stage; then their role is decided, either as possible candidates for a place in the garden, or indeed for a position on a higher stage in the plant world. An encouraging thought at this time is that almost all the new varieties today have come through the same procedure as the one above. Besides, so many more are there to be found in the kaleidoscope of genes, a manipulation of which will bring forth more treasured prizes for the plant breeder.

In the final planting position it is important to consider the right conditions for the variety selected, and always plant deep to offset the dreaded wilt. Once these precautions are taken, then a pleasant future is secured for the new seedling – now all it needs is a name.

F2 SEEDLINGS

When the F1 seedlings are at the flowering stage they should be self-fertilized to create the F2 generation, which will give a far larger variation of plants than the F1 cross did; so to the serious breeder, this stage is clearly necessary. This procedure will give a far wider range of seedlings from which to select the next pairings, the reason for the multiplication of choice being that more recessive genes are brought into visual play, these new genes manifesting themselves in exciting new plants never seen before. These new seedlings can then be back-crossed to the best sister seedling, or indeed back to the best of the parent.

Once a new variety has pleased the grower with its performance, cuttings can be taken to multiply the stock.

Daffodils and Tulips

SIMPLICITY GUIDE

Measure of difficulty	Crossing stage	Flower to seed	Seed germination	Seedling stage
VERY EASY	VERY EASY	EASY	EXPERIENCE	FAIRLY EASY

SITES FOR BEST RESULTS These plants can be grown anywhere in almost any soil.
SPECIAL NOTES Patience is required as these plants take at least four years to flower.

This group is for the connoisseur: these flowers are very simple to crossbreed, but need a lot of patience since it takes five years at least for the first bloom to show its head. After the first blooms appear, and as long as there has been a crossbreeding programme each year, you should have seedlings coming into bloom every season. Many varied types will develop from these crosses, and many of them will be good enough to grow on to make a wonderful show in the garden. To get something special you will need to select the parent plants very carefully – buy the best you can afford, and the newest and best varieties currently on the market. Going to daffodil and tulip shows will give the best insight as to the quality you are aiming for.

Each new daffodil or tulip you see on the show bench was most likely pollinated by the method described here, and it would be at least five years before it showed its first flower, and many more to get the supply of offspring to flowering size. This is why a good variety costs more than most, but to crossbreed you need to have good foundation stock if special new varieties are to be expected. This does not mean you can't use any daffodil to another daffodil or any tulip to another tulip – you can, and good results can be expected, but using the best varieties as parents will give the best chance of creating better class plants and the wonderful flowers we are aiming for.

It is essential to start with healthy bulbs. You can plant bulbs in the garden or in pots, and either way will get good results, although if grown in the greenhouse, pollen will be more plentiful at the time of flowering; also, wet weather at the time of flowering could spoil some of the outside crosses.

THE CROSS

To crossbreed this group, select the flower to be used as the seed-bearing parent, and just before the petals open, prise them apart enough to remove the stamens. As the petals are opened, the trumpet or cup can be parted to get to the vital organs. From the centre of the flower grows the stigma with its

The petals opened to gain access to the stamens.

Removing the stamens with tweezers.

Collecting the pollen using a small brush.

Applying pollen to the stigma.

Ripe seed pod ready to open at the end of June.

three lobes at the tip, and growing very closely alongside this are the six stamens, although on the cup varieties the stamens tend to grow out at the ends. All six stamens must be removed without causing any harm to the stigma. When removed, these stamens can be kept on a saucer or container, and should be kept dry; they can then be used to pollinate another flower. Examine the tip of the stigma, with a magnifying glass if possible; when it is seen to glisten and to have become sticky, apply the pollen from the selected male flower. A warm day is best for this operation because the pollen will be more active at that time. Cover the head for a couple of days just in case a bumblebee decides to call. The seeds will mature when fertilization is complete.

Some time in June the ovary at the base of the flower will swell to its full size; when it turns brown and the stem below the bud begins to wither, take off

Ripe seeds taken from the seed pod. Sow after cleaning.

the head and put it somewhere to dry off. Sometimes the seed rattles loose in the pod: they are jet black, round and easy to handle. Note that if the stem below the seedpod is still green and healthy, then the seeds are still maturing; but as soon as the seeds are ready, the plant stops feeding the bud and the stem dies – this is nature's way of not wasting food and energy.

THE SEED

Sow the ripe young seeds as soon as possible after harvesting. Place them in a sieve and rinse them well in tepid water to remove any inhibitors in the seed coating – these help to prevent germination until the right conditions are available. Soaking in warm water for twenty-four hours helps. Sow in pots if only a few, but in boxes or trays if many are to be sown, and be sure that only sterilized compost of good quality is used or it will be impossible to tell the difference between the grass-like seedlings and weeds, because they stay in this position for two seasons. Cover the soil with small gravel, and the pots or boxes with small-mesh wire netting, to protect from slugs, birds and mice.

After sowing the seeds in their pots, plunge them to the rim in peat or ashes and let the weather look after them; it is very seldom that they need attention, except to make sure the pots don't dry out, and that they are kept safe from mice and birds during the germinating period. In the first season only a small leaf will result, no more than a blade of grass; this dies back at the end of the season and forms a small bulbil. During this period the contractile root action will have pulled the bulbil down in the compost to the correct depth; it sends up two or three leaves the following year. After the second season the small bulbs are planted in a nursery row, making sure that at all times their markers are moved with them. Watch out for birds pulling out the labels: this is a good reason to make a plan of the area and mark in the seedling code numbers.

A weak liquid feed will help the young bulbs to develop once the grass leaves are well established.

When the four-year span is up, any bulb that has reached flowering size will be showing as soon as the winter snows have gone – and how you will gloat over them! After the flower dies down, remove the dead head to prevent the young bulb setting seed; this will help to develop a bigger bulb for the following year, when a bigger, better flower will be worth the wait. If you want to chance a further cross with your seedlings, cross some back to the best parent, some with sister seedlings and some self-pollinated; all these crosses will produce more exciting seedlings. These new bulbs can be grown on to develop more stock of your seedlings, and any that show good promise of being something special can be entered into the daffodil classes to see how they compete with the speciality growers, especially as most of the opposition will be using named varieties. To win a class with your own-bred plant confirms the pedigree of your plants – and proves that as long as the foundation stock was the best available, then the offspring should be on a par with the very finest.

By crossing your best to your best, adding sometimes a new outcross will establish your stock to a very high standard, always producing good quality plants and even the occasional special. It is understandable why the new varieties cost so much, but surely the creator of these wonderful flowers deserves his share of the praise, and the rewards this work can bring.

TULIPS

If tulips are treated in almost the same way as we treat the daffodil, we will get the same positive results. The flower head is rather different, but if the tulip is opened before it opens itself, the stamens can be removed as well as the petals. By removing the petals also, the bees leave the flowers alone; these then can be cross-pollinated with the usually black pollen of the stamens from the flower of your choice, so that the tip of the stigma is fully covered. The stigma has three lobes on the tip, and glistens when ripe. The black pollen is very easy to apply and there is generally enough to cover the tip with ease, so then there is nothing to do except wait for Mother Nature to develop the flower seeds. The ovary at the base of the stigma will swell until the seedpod dominates the tall stem. Leave this in place as long as possible to allow the seed contained inside to ripen, dealing with them in an identical way to the daffodil. There are many different types of tulip, and the majority of them can be crossbred with each other to create some wonderful new varieties.

Open flower showing both the stigma and stamens.

ABOVE: *Applying pollen to the ripe stigma.*

Seed pod developing; treat as for the daffodil.

Dahlias

Measure of difficulty	Crossing stage	Flower to seed	Seed germination	Seedling stage
SKILL NEEDED	TRICKY	FAIRLY EASY	EASY	EASY

SITES FOR BEST RESULTS Open areas, in full sun, gross feeder; it will repay all the attention given.
SPECIAL NOTES Plant in well drained soil, it is not fussy. It will give a good show almost anywhere.

Native to the Mexican region and South America, the dahlia was introduced to Europe in 1789. It was apparently brought to England by Lord Bute from Spain, and was said to be named after the Swedish botanist Dahl. The plants of today are a long way from resembling the plants imported those many years ago. Within a few years more varieties were brought in to satisfy demands for variation; these included *D. variabilis*, which has bright red and purples; *D. coccinca*, another brighter red; and the yellow *D. merckii*.

No special varieties were recorded until seed collector Humbolot sent dahlia seed to England, France and Germany. From the time the seed arrived there was a dramatic change in the development of the dahlia, with many new colours as well as new forms, although singles were in dominance. In fact it wasn't until 1808 that the first double flower was recorded, raised by Hartweg of Karlsrume. You can imagine the excitement the hybridists felt at such a breakthrough, particularly when they considered its potential.

The development of this beautiful flower has been gathering momentum season by season, and a great many varied types have been introduced, such as the cactus and pompoms, as well as the waterlily, giants and the decoratives. Today's breeders seem to be concentrating on exhibition blooms, and if a new variety has little impact on the show bench then it is almost destined for the compost heap. Thus many new varieties are created but only survive in the gardens of those breeders who can penetrate the commercial world with the help of the showmen.

New plants are introduced every year, with many outstanding specimens good enough to be the best variety in the show. But even outstanding individual seedlings take a few seasons to get established, and have to prove themselves before the general public look for, and buy them. Once into that position, however, they are worth their weight in gold. It is amazing that so many varied types can derive from the few ancestors that were their foundation, so much so that even the Dahlia Society have to modify their classification of varieties as the different types appear; but this is the progress we all enjoy and appreciate.

Hybridizing the dahlia is a fascinating pastime, although monetary rewards are also within reach of successful breeders. But the testing of seedlings in the open ground brings so much magic and expectation, particularly when the first flower appears.

SELECTION

At first examination of the plant to be used as a seed parent, it looks an intimidating task; the flower is so full of petals it gives little indication as to where to make a start. It is perhaps better for the beginner to practise on the single type plant, or at least to examine a flower in great detail to familiarize himself with the structure and formation of the stigmas and stamens, the essential organs that need to be manipulated to produce potential winners.

It is easy enough just to gather seed from mature plants that were left to nature's own devices, and take a chance on finding something good in the crop produced. There will be no full pedigree to refer back to, but the majority of the plants will be on the mediocre side. Certainly many exciting newcomers have reached the show bench from this method, nevertheless a more controlled, methodical system is more rewarding.

Start early in the season if an outdoor method is used, so that the seeds so formed have a long season to mature whilst the weather is warm and dry; seed heads of the dahlia have a tendency to rot once the withering flower gets damp.

MAKING A START

The dahlia, as with all daisy-type flowers, has a flower head made up of many tiny florets. In fact every petal is a flower in itself. The outer ones are the ray petals, most of which contain a stigma, these maturing over many days starting from the outer ones and working towards the centre of the bloom; the inner florets are the disc ones that produce the pollen. Many flowers are lacking in both stigma and stamens, as though all their strength has been devoted to the production of these lovely double blooms – also the ones missing the reproductive organs produce the largest tubers. It will be noticed that the stigmas are ripe ahead of the stamens, and some florets have both; but the delay between the two prevents or discourages self-pollination, although this does often happen.

When selection has been made of the plant to be crossbred, start by potting up into not-too-large a pot; and don't feed, just water, with the idea of growing on in poor conditions. The plant will grow more slowly and be less vibrant, so producing smaller, semi-double and maybe single blooms, and this will make the application of pollen much easier; also pollen from such underfed plants will be more plentiful and easily accessible. Nevertheless seed from such a plant will grow into a full sized and normal plant if given the nourishment, and grown in good conditions.

The pollen or male flower can be cut when fully open, or better still when the flower is on the wane. Stand in water to continue to fade, then the stamens will produce lots of pollen from the centre of the bloom and each day more stamens will mature, so giving a good supply of pollen.

Stamens ripe with pollen.

On close inspection of the seed flower, the stigma will be seen deep in the floret. Cut off the floret petal with small scissors just above the stigma; as each day goes by, you will notice the stigma growing above the cut floret, where it will be easy to pollinate as soon as it becomes ripe. A magnifying glass is very useful to see if the stigma is in a sufficiently ripe state to accept the pollen, also that enough has adhered. The petals containing the stigmas actually ripen from the outer ring through to the inner ones, but the process of ripening takes quite a few days until the whole head is complete. This means the pollinating process must be applied every day to make sure that as many stigmas as possible are dealt with.

The main part of the operation is now complete, and protecting the head is all that is required. In a few weeks' time the pod or cluster will show familiar signs of swelling and hopefully an abundance of seed. If the pod takes on a conical shape, which is usual, then all appears well, but check the pod often to make sure that moisture is not held in the seed head, as this sometimes causes the seed to rot. A gentle squeeze between thumb and forefingers will extract any unwanted liquid; this can be a problem when the autumn nights bring a heavy dew.

When the seed can be felt in the firm plump head, the stem can be cut to a length of at least 25cm (10in) and stood in a container of water, either indoors or in the greenhouse, to fully ripen the seed. When the head is really dry, the seed can be removed from the chaff and placed on a tray to

Showing the petals removed to show stigmas at the base of each petal.

dry thoroughly, then put into a paper bag for a few weeks before being stored until sowing time in the spring. These black or grey seeds will carry your hopes for the following season.

SEED SOWING

When to sow the seed depends very much on the conditions in which they are intended to grow. If a greenhouse with enough heat to keep out the frosts is available, then an early start in late February or

Old flower petals are removed to show the ripe pollen in the disc centre.

Harvesting the ripe seeds. Keep them dry to be sown in the spring.

Seedlings at the pricking out stage. Keep labels with the seedlings.

early March can be contemplated. If only a cold frame is to be used, then April will be a safer period. To sow outdoors is best left until late May. The earlier the start, the more quickly the first flower will appear, and all hybridists look forward more than anything else to the opening of the first new flower. From an early start in the greenhouse the seedlings will be in a very advanced stage by planting out time in late May or early June, depending where you live.

Sow the seed in good seed compost, water in, then cover with either glass or clingfilm. Shading with newspaper can be helpful, but it must be removed at the first sign of germination, which can be as early as eight to ten days. If the seed is well spaced out at sowing time, potting on becomes a simple operation. Seedlings can be transplanted into 8cm (3½in) pots using a more nutritious compost; from here they will then be transferred to their flowering position, at a safe time when frosts are finally over.

SEEDLING SELECTION

When the seedlings are in full bloom you will notice the different colours, which usually appear in the F1 stage. It is possible to have differing types of growth – I remember having several decoratives, some cactus and a pompom in the same batch of seedlings from the same cross. Most of the seedlings were destined for the compost heap, but two became very

good plants with lovely blooms. It must be expected that a large proportion of the offspring will lack the qualities required, but by sifting through and eliminating all but the top class type plants, then a good foundation will begin to appear.

This is the time to assess the quality of the offspring: are the seedlings from this cross worthy of keeping to use as a back-cross to the best parent? Are they better than their parents, or indeed showing something new, perhaps in the colour or type of plant, that is superior to their parents? These are the decisions to make if any young plants are to take their place in the breeding programme. Although many different colours can surface from a first-time cross, it can be noted that by back-crossing a seedling the same colour as the parent, the resulting seedlings will have a high percentage of that colour, and the type will also tend towards the seed parent. It goes without saying that this line of approach should be abandoned if only inferior seedlings appear, and another pairing should be selected to try again. If this line proves a winning one, then continue in this direction to develop the qualities that already exist. As mentioned before, start with quality stock to give a flying start.

If you are fortunate enough to breed something special, then compare the plant alongside an established variety. Or compete in your local flower show, not only to show off your prize possession, but to test its quality against good opposition.

Delphiniums

SIMPLICITY GUIDE

Measure of difficulty	Crossing stage	Flower to seed	Seed germination	Seedling stage
FAIRLY EASY	TRICKY	EASY	READ METHOD	EASY

SITES FOR BEST RESULTS Borders, open areas, but not in dark shady spots; full sun, will tolerate dappled shade.
SPECIAL NOTES Stake if planted on windy sites. They are prone to slug and snail damage, especially in the seedling stage.

There are some beautiful spikes of this magnificent border plant already in existence, and a newcomer to plant breeding may consider it an impossible task to attempt to better the impressive blooms of today. It has a powerful range of colours, from whites, creams and pinks to a full spectrum of blues, and the reds are due to make an appearance any time now.

It is a plant almost beyond recognition when compared to the true wild delphinium species from whence it came. Some of these species were used to help advance the modern varieties, such as *D. elatum* that originated high in the colder regions of the Alps and Siberia, and another from Siberia was *D. cheilanthum*. Also adding their genetic contributions were species *D. grandiflorum* and *D. tatsienense*, and other wild species were undoubtedly used to procure the wonderful varieties that we now possess.

Although by the seventeenth century many hybrids were available, it wasn't until the eighteenth and nineteenth centuries that any considerable progress was made; particularly noteworthy is Lemoine in France for his 'Statuaire Rude', and James Kelway for his 'King of the Delphiniums'. Another great contribution to the status of this majestic plant was supplied by the amalgamation of the famous Blackmore and Langdon nurseries which up to the present time have provided many wonderful prize-winning spikes, combined with an outstanding colour range. Frank Bishop is another important delphinium breeder: rated an amateur before joining Bakers nursery, he has listed many outstanding varieties to his name. He has always admitted a soft spot for his 'Mrs Frank Bishop', but one of his finest contributions to the delphinium world must be his 'Swan Lake', which was the outstanding variety of its day.

Mention must also be made of Watkin Samuel who resided in Wrexham and was the creator of the 'Wrexham Hybrids'. These plants were shown in 1921 at the RHS show, and created a stir because of their huge spikes that grew to 3m (9ft) or more. You can imagine the difficulty trying to save these giants from the strong winds we sometimes suffer. Today's trend is for spikes that are not so tall, and with a more manageable height, the vigour required to produce such monumental spikes has been channelled into the creation of florets that are large and beautifully formed.

The hallmark of the modern period is the fascination with the red delphinium, and gigantic steps have been made in fixing the colours of red, orange and deep pinks. Now all that remains to be accomplished is a more robust constitution. Although spikes and individual florets have achieved much greater size, an improvement in vigour and general constitution is still in the building process. These are the plants that future generations will consider an everyday type of delphinium and we can look forward to a mixed border of reds, whites, pinks and blues.

Most of today's top varieties originate from the skills of the amateur, and generally find their way onto the open market via the nurseries who introduce

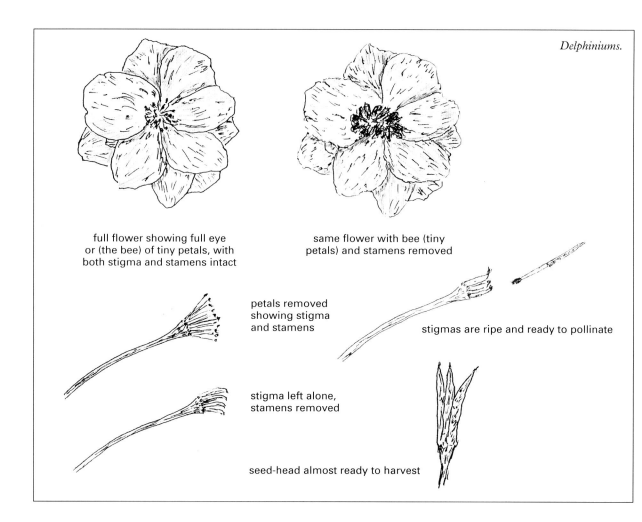

Delphiniums.

full flower showing full eye
or (the bee) of tiny petals, with
both stigma and stamens intact

same flower with bee (tiny
petals) and stamens removed

petals removed
showing stigma
and stamens

stigmas are ripe and ready to pollinate

stigma left alone,
stamens removed

seed-head almost ready to harvest

the specials to the public. The breeding of delphiniums is indeed a fascinating occupation, whether to fulfil a hobby, or for purely horticultural needs. Many outstanding varieties have arisen from random crosses by nature herself, helped by the endeavours of the bees and insects; but the fact remains, the best of the varieties today have come about through the patient manipulations of the plant breeder.

Some idea of the type of plant required is necessary to guide the breeder to success in the final product. And even when this is created to his satisfaction, it is not the end of proceedings, because he will then endeavour to cross this special to another quality plant to achieve something even better. Maybe perfection is beyond our capabilities, but in trying, step by step, to achieve it we encounter so

many thrills and surprises, and this alone makes the effort rewarding.

Everyone has a different perception as to the type of plant they want to create, but most growers have at least an idea of the more general trend by visiting flower shows. Even so, the fascination with variety is reflected in the achievements of our fellow breeders.

PARENT SELECTION

Selecting the parents may sound an easy matter, but not all plants fall into the same category. For the seed-bearing parent, select the one that has the capability to setting plenty of seed. Not all plants of the delphinium family are generous in this

The ideal stage to open and remove stamens.

growth, strength of stem and well spaced florets that touch, giving the impression of a solid pillar.

Many of the qualities adorning the parent could be the backbone of your future seedling, though bear in mind that unfavourable characteristics will more than likely also end up as part of the plant. It is therefore a false economy to use even one inferior plant. Nevertheless, a batch of seedlings from good quality stock is almost certain to include one special seedling. Selection of colours is a personal choice.

Newcomers to crossbreeding delphiniums may find it helpful to take a floret from a plant and pull it to pieces on a table in order to study it more closely, and become better acquainted with the sexual parts we need to manipulate. If you do this, compare your findings with the line drawings on page 44: this will help you to understand the procedure ahead, and this method of emasculation will explain things more clearly than words.

HOW TO MAKE THE CROSS

Select a floret at the stage of beginning to open, and gently pluck off the petals with an outward tug, making sure that all parts are removed. Once these have gone it will also be possible to pull away the eye petals known as the 'bee', surrounding the stigmas and the unwanted stamens. These are usually of a

department, and some offer none whatsoever; furthermore, lack of pollen is another problem with some plants. Flowers inadequate in producing pollen are usually the ones showing off huge florets, but this qualification can be helpful if this plant is used as the seed-bearing parent. Use plants that are close to your ideal, and look for vigorous

contrasting colour intended to attract the bees to the centre of the flower. The next step is to remove the stamens, making absolutely certain that no anthers have released their pollen; the stigmas at this stage are immature and not ready for pollination, but they are very easily damaged, and great care is needed in this emasculation of the flower. The stigmas at this stage are small and immature, needing two days or more to reach the point of pollination. As that stage is reached the stigmas will have extended a little, and opened wide at the tips exposing a sticky coating: this is the time to place pollen from the selected male plant onto the stigmas.

There are several ways of introducing pollen from the male flower: perhaps the most convenient is plucking the flower from the plant, removing the bee (the centre petals) and dusting the seed parent stigmas with the pollen-laden flower. As our British climate can be unpredictable, a second and third coating of pollen on succeeding days is a good insurance to successful pollination. Before leaving the plant, mark the floret with the details of the parentage and records of the pedigree. A helpful method of labelling is to tie coloured cotton onto the floret stem and mark the label accordingly that is placed in the soil – any weight other than cotton on the floret would break it off.

Showing the developing seed pods.

HARVEST TIME

Seedpods will ripen in six to eight weeks, so keep a careful watch against birds in particular causing damage. When the pods darken in colour from green to brown is an indication of their ripe condition. Make a point of collecting the pods before they burst; place the whole pods in paper bags to dry in a warm place, such as on a windowsill.

SEED SOWING

Sow fresh seed soon after harvesting for the best germinating results; though this method is only to be recommended if warmth against the cold frost of winter can be given. Another problem to guard against is damping off disease, a fungus that affects the stems of the seedlings when they are very

Almost ripe seedpods. Make sure you harvest before the pods burst open.

Ripe black seed showing in the burst seed pods.

young. It is highly infectious, and once a seedling succumbs to this disease it can spread through the whole box of seedlings. The best way to protect them is to use only the purest of compost, and water with a fungicide liquid. They normally stay in a dormant state or develop very slowly until the spring, so don't worry if they lose all their leaves and look dead, but look after them, because nine times out of ten they send up new leaves when the warmer and lighter days of spring bring them to life; then they will be off to a flying start, showing off their magnificent spikes in the same summer.

Note that a better plant will be encouraged if the spike of the seedling is cut off as it appears above ground in its first season; it will then put all its strength into building a robust plant for the following year. As an alternative to this summer sowing, the seed can be harvested, dried a little longer, then placed in a sealed container and kept in a cold place, or even the fridge. Germinating times can vary with different varieties, generally ranging from four days to three weeks, although reluctant strains can take months. These 'delayed' species require a cold spell before emerging, which is closer to their natural growing conditions.

To grow a few seeds, a well tested method is to fold several layers of kitchen roll paper onto a small tray (Chinese take-away is ideal). Soak with cool, boiled water, leaving 6mm (¼in) in the bottom. The thickness of the paper keeps the seeds lying on the top, up above the water line so they are always damp but never wet. Lie the seed on the paper, then place one single sheet on top of the seeds; this will soak up the moisture and keep them damp. Cover with clingfilm, then place in a cool dark place in the summer, or at 15°C (60°F) in early spring. Examine them each day from the third day, removing each one as it germinates, and sowing it in a small pot of good quality compost; grow them on for a few days in the same temperature until established. This will give the seedlings a wonderful start, and a good germination can be expected.

When using the traditional method of pots or trays, use only good quality compost. Soak the compost well before placing the seed on the surface and lightly pressing into the soil. Cover with the slightest dusting of soil or sand, then place in a dark, cool position as suggested above.

SEEDLING DEVELOPMENT

As the seedlings develop, they need to be situated where the light is good, to keep them short and sturdy. If they are grown in a greenhouse it is essential to shade them from the sun, as they are tender and will burn. In a few weeks' time the true leaves will appear, and three weeks after this the seedlings will be ready to transplant into pots. They can then grow on in the same environment until they are well rooted in the pots, when they will need to be acclimatized to outdoor conditions.

The best time to plant out the seedlings into their permanent position is in April or May, though inevitably this will depend entirely on the ground conditions at the time; if conditions are good, they will grow at a tremendous rate. With perfect conditions the flowers will show their fineries in late summer, although the size will be smaller for the first season.

SEEDLING SELECTION

The most exciting time is when the flowers open on the first spike from your previous year's pairings. As they all develop the quality of your selected crossings will become apparent, though if room is no

Seedlings under trial.

problem, then most can be given their second year trial, which should give a clear indication as to your progress. Study each plant individually and assess not only its attributes, but also its undesirable characteristics, to finish with a complete evaluation of the cross as a whole. This will be the F1 generation. From the findings, the seedlings showing the best overall qualities can go forward to the F2 stage, from where there are three different options.

THE F2 GENERATION

To take the seedlings to the F2 stage, try to self-cross the best of the seedlings back to themselves by the same process as before, but using pollen from a different floret on the same plant; this will release the recessive genes into the F2 seedlings,

and will throw up a combination of previously hidden characteristics. This process will supply more variations for the next stage, unless a special variety appears at this early phase, which is quite feasible and can be expected.

The next method is to back-cross to the best of the two parents: this will highlight and substantiate any qualities present in the breeding line – not forgetting that undesirable traits could follow the same pattern. Finally, crossing the best two seedlings will emphasize the better qualities present in the genetic make-up of the line.

All these methods will bring some of the recessive characteristics to the surface, and something completely different from your present stock. Whether they are better than their parents, or even as good, may depend on your breeding techniques and the kindness of Lady Luck.

Fuchsias

Measure of difficulty	Crossing stage	Flower to seed	Seed germination	Seedling stage
EASY	EASY	EASY	BE TOLERANT	EASY

SITES FOR BEST RESULTS Greenhouse in early stages, anywhere in the garden after the frosts, likes good fertile soil and is a gross feeder.

SPECIAL NOTES By stopping as suggested, a perfect plant will be achieved. Good open compost, good drainage and regular feeding. When the seedlings are stopped for the first time, take a cutting and allow to grow on to flower. This will soon bloom before the seedling to show the colour, shape and so on.

The fuchsia plant is not only one of the prettiest in cultivation, it also adapts well to very varied growing conditions. There is a range of varieties, responding to any growing method – indeed, very few species of plant can offer the diversity of beauty possessed by this amazing family of exuberant flowers. The first recorded sightings were in the area of the Dominican Republic; amongst these the variety *F. tryphilla flore coccinea* was found by Father Charles Plumier. He named it after an admired botanist Leonard Fuchs in 1703, and it was thought to be the only type of its kind in existence.

Throughout the next fifty years there must have been many other sightings of different species, but there were no records until 1788, when Kew Gardens were gifted a plant referred to as *F. coccinea*. More plants soon followed, and it was only a matter of time before the nurserymen of the day produced different variations from the many plants found. Wealthy plantsmen soon went out looking for new species, to be found throughout South America.

Today the variety of plants is truly huge, created by the crossing of different species throughout the world, and giving the hybridist a whole kaleidoscope of ideas. So many combinations are available that a close scrutiny of the different types is needed, so as to plan out exactly what you are aiming for. The better the foundation plan as to the crosses you will need will bring you closer to

the realization of your ideal than any haphazard application of pollen. The fuchsia stays close to the parentage type, and a quality parent is more likely to produce quality seedlings. There is a deviation from the type on occasion, but invariably mediocre specimens are the result, these almost certainly created by inferior recessive genes that appear in the make-up of the seedling from way back in the genetic ancestry of the parents. This shows why it is so important to select high class varieties as parents.

Most fuchsia plants have the natural beauty of the species, but close scrutiny of some varieties will reveal many faults, particularly in the corolla. This part of the flower is important when assessing quality, but the flaws are not always obvious, and only examination will reveal the faults. Many corollas are split or uneven, and this is evident in every flower of that variety, but the faults are masked by the overwhelming profusion of imperfect blooms, and from a distance the plant is certainly very beautiful.

PARENTAL SELECTION

Before selecting the proposed parents, examine each for perfect formation, not only in the blooms, but also in their growth habit; in particular the stems between the leaf nodes should be short, as

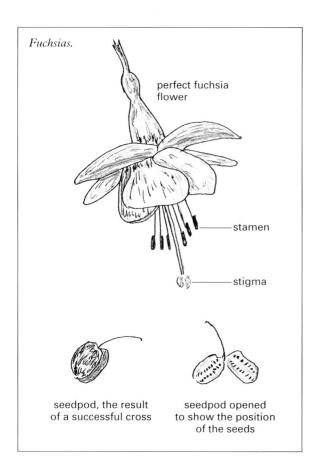

Fuchsias.

perfect fuchsia flower

stamen

stigma

seedpod, the result of a successful cross

seedpod opened to show the position of the seeds

the first and most important part is the ovary: this is the womb of the plant, and produces the seed for our next generation. The tube is attached to the ovary and is mainly the protection cover plus the base of the main flower parts; at the base inside is the nectar that attracts the bees to enter the flower to assist in pollination. The sepals are the wings of the upper part covering the petaloids and the corolla.

THE CROSS

Start by using a flower that is just opening, or one that can be popped open; at this stage the stamens are immature, and the pollen is still held inside the anthers. These stamens holding the anthers can be removed with a small pair of scissors or small tweezers, though make sure the stigma is not harmed – at this point it may be at the sticky stage, when it is ripe for pollination. This is sometimes apparent immediately, but if it is still dry it can be left until the next day, which is often the case.

If conducting proceedings outdoors, then a paper bag over the flower will prevent interference from

this will reduce the chances of long, gangling stems. Check also the florescence structure, which on some plants produces an abundance of flowers. If all these qualities can be found, and if like is used with like, then success is just around the corner.

Although the cross can be made in the open ground, it may be better to proceed using potted plants indoors or in the comfort of a greenhouse; certainly there will be less interference from insects and bees, making for a more certain intended cross.

THE FLOWER

It is essential to study the make-up of the bloom before beginning the reproduction stage. This is quite an easy flower to deal with, but examining and identifying the parts will make the crossbreeding task much simpler. Working down from the stem,

Bud in ideal condition to be opened to cross-pollinate.

The petals are removed to show the stigma and stamens.

Flower opened. Stamens removed leaving the stigma clear of pollen.

unwanted intruders, unless the complete corolla is taken off, in which case the bloom will be attractive to insect callers. Working in a greenhouse will not require these precautions, nor will the weather be a nuisance. The reason for using an unopened bloom to start with is to be sure that no insect or bee has been there before you. Application of the pollen is easy, and the results are obvious to the naked eye; if the stigma is ripe, the pollen will adhere very well, and a good coating can be made. Sometimes when a stamen is stroked onto the stigma, the pollen comes onto it like cotton wool and can be wrapped around the sticky surface; naturally this varies, however, and it can be very dust-like in its application. It is a worthwhile practice to apply the pollen to the stigma on several occasions on successive days, to be sure of catching the stigma in prime condition.

The next stage will be the drying of the stigma tip: this turns from a cream-coloured, sticky-coated lobe to a brown, dried-up stem, which is good news if it is fertilized, but bad news if nothing has taken place. The development of the berry does not always mean success: some varieties develop some lovely big berries, but are filled with liquid and only empty seed shells and some with only a suggestion of seed, but let them mature regardless until the time when they are opened to reveal their contents. It is possible to find one solitary seed in a huge berry, which makes searching through them all worth the trouble. The good seeds are obvious to see as they are solid and easily removed from the pulp: by pressing the pod onto a piece of kitchen paper, or by feeling with the finger tip, the moisture enters the paper and the seed is felt beneath the finger and is removed onto another clean sheet.

After removal, place them in a tea strainer and rinse them under a slow-running tap (put the plug in the sink); place a basin under the strainer. With the finger tip, gently but firmly, twirl the seeds around the strainer; this will release the remainder of the pulp, and any inhibitors still adhering to the seed. Tap the seeds onto a clean sheet of paper; these are then dried, and are ready to sow when the time comes.

Ripe seed pods ready to be harvested.

BELOW: *Seedlings planted out. Note the growth space allowed.*

THE SEED

If the seeds feel hard and firm to the fingertip, then these are usually perfect; many may be soft, and these are more likely to be empty cases. Select only the firm type to save wasting time on rubbish. For seed compost, use any good, reliable brand; mix it with 30 per cent sharp sand, firmed down and then watered with cool, boiled water. Sprinkle the seeds on the surface; do not cover them but gently press them into the compost. Gently spray them with more cooled, boiled water with a fungicide added in case the seed itself is infected. Don't forget to label with the appropriate pedigree, then cover the pot with clingfilm ready to place in the propagator at a temperature of 16–19°C (60–67°F).

If the seed is sown as soon as it is ripe, a better germination can be expected, and seedlings should start to show in three to four weeks time. Grow on in the pots until the second leaf stage, when they can be potted singly into starter pots. At the fourth

pair of leaves, take out the tip of the seedling to make the plant bush out from the three remaining pairs of leaves, giving six stems on the bush. After two pairs of leaves have grown on the six stems, nip out the tips again. This makes a bush with twenty-four stems to produce your new seedling: they will quickly fill the pots with roots, but provided they are moved on before they become pot-bound, they will grow very quickly. This method produces flowers later, but meanwhile it is a perfect plant to analyse and study, to help decide if it has enough quality to keep.

Most breeders want to see the flowers as quickly as possible, and the answer is to pot up the first tip taken from the seedling and let it grow as it pleases. This rooted tip cutting will flower long before the seedling it came from, and the breeder will have the satisfaction of knowing the type of flower to expect on the well developed seedling.

Many cuttings can be taken if the seedling proves to be something special, and these will provide the

Seedlings showing the variation between them, although all come from the same pod.

BELOW: *The colour and shape variation from seedlings from the same pod.*

next stage to back-cross to the best of the parents. By doing this the quality characteristics in both the seedling and the parent can be bonded to become a dominant trait in the family line. A good solid framework, with short internodes, healthy foliage and an abundance of well held, perfect blooms is the ideal to aim for, and with patience and plenty of endeavour the results can be only a few crosses away.

The type of plant grown is the choice of the breeder; some prefer the flamboyant, showy doubles, and others the singles that provide many more flowers per stem. Some have a liking for the species, and all can be accommodated from the selection of types available. Note that the first year seedlings tend to be of the type of the seed parent, but colours are always varied.

Gladioli

Measure of difficulty	Crossing stage	Flower to seed	Seed germination	Seedling stage
VERY EASY	VERY EASY	VERY EASY	QUITE EASY	EASY

SITES FOR BEST RESULTS Borders; any position away from shade will produce perfect plants.
SPECIAL NOTES The seedling will flower in its second year. Cut off the flower before it develops to allow the baby corm to mature.

This is a wonderful flower to hybridize: even the weakest seedling would still make a spectacular plant in the border. Many can be positively mediocre as F1 offspring, but there is still the likelihood of some spectacular seedlings, especially in the F2 generation. Thus not only is this plant enthusiastically manipulated by the specialist because of the good specimens that may be acquired, but it is also a beginner's dream of a plant because it is so simple to hybridize.

Modern gladioli have been procured from a combination of several species, most of them from the African continent, particularly South and East Africa. They must also have been from around the Middle East area, as they have been mentioned in the Holy Land in the days of the Romans. Mention was also made by a Greek physician named Dioscorides to 'corn lilies', thought to be gladioli, in the year AD50.

Very little was recorded from these early days until around 1826 when a hybrid was introduced and named after the raiser G. Colville; this, and several others to appear later, were used to procure more exciting types. A man named Hooker of Bletchley raised the bright vermilion/red variety, *Gladiolus bletchleyensis*, and from these exciting new varieties came many new ones. It was thought at this time that the yellow gladioli was as elusive as the yellow sweet pea or the blue rose is today, until one arrived from south-east Africa: the yellow *Gladiolus primulinus*. This species was pale lemon in colour, and the upper petal was formed like a hood, as if protecting the stamens from the downpours in the rainforests and the misty waters from Victoria Falls. It is recorded as being sent from the Zambezi area by Mr Francis Fox in the year 1902.

This encouraged the production of more wonderful varieties, and two of the main specialist firms to take on the production of these plants were Messrs Kelway of Langport, Somerset, and Messrs Unwins of Histon, Cambridge. Many new names of the day were attributed to their skill and dedication, and they undoubtedly gave a wonderful start to the marvellous selection we enjoy today.

MAKING THE CROSS

To the hybridist, and especially the beginner, the gladioli and the lily are ideal plants to start with: simple to fertilize, with the easiest flower structure to manipulate, and a comfortable height at which to carry out the work of pollination and labelling.

Selection of the parent varieties will always be a personal decision by the crossbreeder, but many crucial factors must be checked before the final choice is made. First, consider the strengths of both plants, and select them only if good qualities are to be found in both parents; the policy of some breeders is to cross all and sundry in the hope of 'hitting the jackpot' with at least one of them. Certainly this method will give plenty of seedlings to select from, but there is no way of telling which pairing a good seedling came from, so as to back-cross to the best parent. This F2 cross is vital as regards assessing the quality of the parents as well as the offspring, and without a structured method, no planned pedigree can be maintained. Better to have fewer crosses, but ones that are planned and recorded, for a good harvest of quality seedlings.

THE CROSS

As the spikes grow rapidly upwards, select from the seed parent the bottom floret just before the flower opens; this is the right time to emasculate it. Prise open the petals to reveal the unripe stamens, and take these off, either with small scissors or tweezers, leaving the stigma intact and pollen free. To protect the stigma from bees it can be pinned back to the top petal by a toothpick or matchstick: insert this from behind the top petal by the side of the stigma, passing in front of it and then back into the petal – this will hold the stigma back and should keep it safe from the bees. The next step in the operation is to collect pollen from the male flower.

The stigma will show it is ready when its tip opens into three prongs. Usual practice is to take two stamens from the open male flower, and stroke the ripe pollen onto the stigma of the female flower – as long as the three-pronged stigma is sufficiently sticky to hold the pollen; and if it isn't today, then tomorrow is the day to pollinate. After application, the stigma can be pinned back to keep it safe from contact with the pollen-carrying bee, as mentioned earlier; alternatively, place a paper bag over the floret for a couple of days. Then it is up to Mother Nature to fertilize and ripen the seedpods. Label at once, because although you may think you will remember, as time goes by you won't, and it is frustrating to see all your seedpods looking identical, and being unable to identify the ones you thought you would be sure to remember. No doubt we have all suffered such a catastrophe!

HARVESTING THE SEED

After a few days the seedpod will show signs of development, and then a decision can be made as

The ideal bud to emasculate.

The bud opened to show the stigma and stamens.

to whether to leave the other florets on, or take them off. If the plant is a vigorous one, leave the other florets to flourish, only taking them off if the plant is not so robust, so as to channel all the energies of the plant back into the formation of its seeds. From the time of the cross to the time the ripe pod bursts is roughly six weeks, naturally depending on the weather during this period. Leave the pods on the stems as long as possible, keeping an eye on the ripening process. When they are well ripened, the stem can be cut off and placed on a sheet of paper to dry off on, for instance, a windowsill. The seed is very light, and any gust of wind may blow it away, so take any necessary precautions to keep it safe when dry, until it is time to sow it.

When the pods finally burst open, many dozens of seeds will be available, looking like cornflakes with a darkened centre. If a single seed is held up to a light the actual embryo can be seen between the flaky wafer; those that contain no embryo at all can be discarded. When packing away this valuable harvest, remember to place the pedigree label in with the seed ready for sowing in the spring.

SOWING THE SEED

Although the seed can be sown immediately it is harvested, which naturally gives a very early start, problems arise when the young seedlings must be kept growing through the winter. This entails a heated greenhouse or conservatory, and without either of these it is more realistic to sow in late February or early March.

For good sowing conditions, the ideal is to have a box 15cm (6in) deep, with good rich soil for the bottom 5cm (2in), potting compost for the next 5cm and for the upper 5cm a mixture of sharp sand and fresh seed compost. These conditions bring out the best in the young plants, the top layer to give a gentle start to germination, the middle layer to maintain a steady level of feed to promote excellent development, and finally the richer bottom layer to take the plants through to the autumn. At this stage they will be fully developed, and will stay in the boxes, to be brought indoors during the winter to rest with the older corms until springtime again.

An alternative to the box method, especially if only a few seeds from each cross are to be grown, is to put the same soil mixture into a large pot, sowing the seed 2.5cm (1in) deep. To give the seeds a flying start, keep them in the greenhouse with gentle heat to begin with, gradually hardening them off until the spring, when they will go outside. It is crucial to keep the compost from drying out, especially in hot weather, since a check in growth at any stage will be detrimental to the development of the cormlets.

Yet another way to sow the seeds, especially for the breeder without any heating arrangements – apart from sowing later and growing in the boxes outside totally – is to dig out a drill on a good piece of ground, apply a liberal supply of sandy soil to a depth of 5cm (2in) and sow the seeds 2.5cm (1in) deep, when perfect results can be expected. A general liquid feed during the growing period will pay handsome dividends. Lift the cormlets in the autumn, label them, and store them for the winter.

Note that only a gentle heat is required to start the seed of the gladioli germinating; high temperatures tend to send the seeds into a deep dormancy, and the results can only lead to disappointment.

PLANTING THE BABY CORMLETS

In spring, the ground must be fully prepared for planting the new cormlets. Some will surprise you by the size of the corm in the first year; however, where there is a variation of sizes, do not discard the tiny ones as these often turn out to be the paler colours, whereas the larger ones tend to be strong colours. In the seedlings' second year the larger ones can be expected to throw up their first flower spike, whilst the smaller corms will not show until the following year.

On ripening, corms – even the small ones – often develop tiny cormlets fixed to their base; these will grow into an identical plant to the corm it was attached to in every characteristic way.

Continue to feed the plants through the season even after the flower spike has died back or has been picked, to assist the development of the new cormlets; feeding during this period is essential to build the flower spike embryo to produce next year's spike. After flowering, the main corm tends to break up into many smaller cormlets. If these are saved under the same names, then good supplies of stock can be accumulated.

If you remove the flower as it appears through the leaves on the first year, you will be rewarded with a greater sized corm for a full bloom on its second year. For the majority of the cormlets, the natural flowering time will be the second season, but if seeds are sown each year, then some new flowers are also appearing each year.

The seedlings about 15cm (6in) high.

BELOW: *The seedlings grown in the pots, second year.*

BACK-CROSSING

The first flower from the new seedlings will be some indication as to the quality of your selections; this is the first stage, hopefully, to your ultimate goal. The better seedlings can be expected from a back-cross to the better of the two parent plants; this is not only desirable, but a 'must'. In my experience the better seedlings appear from the F2 and F3 generations, whether these are from crossing best seedling to best parent, or crossing the two best seedlings. In addition, take the self seed from the F1 seedling to produce its own F2: the better colours, and stabilizing of the attributes, will be forthcoming in this generation. Note, too, that faulty characteristic genes could also be multiplied if in evidence, which is why it is so important to select good parents at the outset.

BUILDING STOCK

Feed the plants through the summer to build a fair size corm, giving a potash feed in the autumn to improve the plant's stamina. At lifting time, after all the foliage has died down, lift the corm gently with a fork, shaking off most of the soil as you do so. Look for any cormlets attached, and keep these, as they will be identical to the parent. Label them as usual.

The method of saving the cormlets that are developed from the main corm is the only way in which a breeder can build stock of the chosen variety. Cormlets can be planted in rows in a nursery border with plenty of potting grit to allow for good drainage; a liquid feed will assist in the development of a large, healthy corm.

Heathers

SIMPLICITY GUIDE

Measure of difficulty	Crossing stage	Flower to seed	Seed germination	Seedling stage
VERY DIFFICULT	VERY DIFFICULT	FAIRLY EASY	SLOW BUT GOOD	FAIRLY EASY

SITES FOR BEST RESULTS Any area where the soil is on the acid side with good drainage, although some varieties will tolerate a low percentage of lime.

SPECIAL NOTES When watering or dampening the seed compost, use only lime-free water. Boiled, then cooled rainwater is perfect. Keep seedlings away from hot sun.

Heathers are very popular plants today. They are mainly used to create a lovely, colourful bed of weed-suppressing plants, since they show colour in both flowers and foliage all the year round; they also require little maintenance to keep them in top class condition. Interplanted with dwarf conifers, they are one of the most popular bedding plants in the modern gardening approach, and always look classy. There are many variations within the different species, as well as many different varieties, and this gives a wide range of choice; furthermore, most of the colours change as the new foliage appears, then more colours appear as the flowers burst open along the many stems.

The three most popular species are Erica, Calluna and Daboecia, but there are many hybrid varieties that consist of crossings between these main species, making the heather family as a whole a very large and wonderful group. By using a full range of varieties, it is possible to have colour throughout every month of the year – not an achievement that many plants can match!

The heathers are easy plants to grow, requiring well drained, open, lime-free, acid conditions; if grown in this environment, then good results can be expected. There are some varieties that are tolerant of lime, but these are in the minority, and this capacity is usually mentioned on the labels of heathers sold at garden centres. One important fact of management to remember is to water

Some lovely varieties are available to crossbreed.

heathers with rainwater only: this is because most tapwater contains lime, and its use will cause the loss of many plants.

CROSSING

Many new varieties have their beginnings in the heather beds from seeds that dropped from the hybrid plants onto the perfect growing conditions beneath the parent plants. Examine beneath the plants in the heather bed and look for heather seedlings in the compost below the plants: sometimes the surprise seedling will be found. If it came from one of the species plants, then the seedling would be of that species and would look almost identical to it. However, it could be a cross from a hybrid, even a self-cross, in which case the seedling would be a new variety, though not necessarily a special. Even so, rather than consigning it to the compost heap as a useless nondescript, there is always a chance that it does have something special and is worth growing on – in which case plenty of cuttings can be taken. This might be called the 'random find' method, which produces more inferior plants than the quality ones we are looking for – but nevertheless many top class varieties have arrived using this approach.

A great deal of patience is required to crossbreed heathers, mainly because they are very tiny to operate on, but also because many of the seedlings will not be worth a second glance. Thus you might have a whole row of seedlings in their second year in the hope of a potential winner, but find none as good as the parent plants, and this is very disappointing – but then you might come across one gleaming special in amongst a hundred seedlings, and this makes all the effort and care in producing it worthwhile.

To make this subject more fascinating, any attempt to crossbreed the various colours in the hope of getting something new and special will create a very wide variety of foliage as well as flowers. Many will be poor, but some will be worth growing on for a couple of years, to let the winter and spring bring out the colours in the foliage. On this first cross the seedlings will be more like their parents: this will be the F1 generation. If the plants are allowed to self-seed, this will bring out any recessive traits, thus creating new types and variations; crossing the seedling back to the best parent or sister seedling will also bring out hidden characteristics, to help develop something new. These seeds will come under the category of F2 generation.

The young plant ideal to cross with.

The plant in flower.

To get to the F2 or F3 generation can take two or three years, but by then you will have a worthwhile foundation and more than likely something extra special, an objective worth achieving.

Make a thorough survey of your stock plants to decide in which direction you wish to progress, whether you want a more brilliant foliage, better and bigger flowers, softer tones, upright or prostrate habit: it is just as well to have an objective, and attempt to achieve it by crossing the correct varieties. However, before any attempt at crossbreeding this flower, it might be a helpful exercise to take off a stem of flowers and examine a floret under a strong light with a magnifying glass, to familiarize yourself with its constituent parts. Gently pull open a flower with a pair of tweezers: the stigma and stamens will be quite easy to distinguish. Furthermore one floret is almost identical to all other flowers, so once you have studied the construction of one, if you can deal with that one, then you will be able to tackle all the range.

Select a young unopened flower from the spray.

THE CROSS

To make the cross, choose your seed parent – the seedlings will mostly resemble this one in the F1 generation – and emasculate the smallest floret that has not yet opened, by very carefully tearing down the tube or bell to reveal the stigma and stamens. Examine it closely with the magnifying glass to make sure that no pollen has been released, then proceed to take off all the stamens, leaving the undamaged stigma. If at least two florets on the same stem can be treated this way, then all the others on the stem can be taken off; this leaves just the two lone stigmas, making it easier for you to check progress. Pollen from the other selected parent plant can now be applied to the tips of the stigmas; make sure that some pollen stays in place by checking with the magnifying glass afterwards. Mark the stem with the names of the parents, and the date by tying coloured cotton on the floret and taking notes. When looking for pollen from the male plant it will be noticed that the stamens on a fully open floret will show above the flower tube, and are usually of a contrasting colour, which adds to the beauty of the species. It may be wise to cover the stem

LEFT: *Single flower to show how to emasculate.*

MIDDLE: *Single flower with petals removed, showing stigma and stamens.*

RIGHT: *Only the stigma left ready to be pollinated.*

with a bag to stop intruders for a few days, although with the petals removed, insects, and particularly bees, don't show any interest.

Two days later, you should apply pollen again to make pollination more certain and even a third application is not out of the question. It is worth taking this extra trouble to guarantee the result.

The most important point in all this operation is to catch the stigma before any other pollen reaches it, being careful not to bruise or damage the stigma in any way; following this method you can be almost certain of some seed.

Keep an eye on your marked cross because it needs to be protected until the seed is ripe. To help in deciding the time to harvest, check other plants of the same type in the vicinity by shaking the flower heads over a clean sheet of white paper: if ready, the very tiny seeds, almost like dust, will be visible. Then cut off the stem of your cross and very carefully place it in a paper bag before shaking out your special seed.

SOWING THE SEED

The seed is best sown as soon as it is ripe, as it has a short life. Sow in pots using special ericaceous lime-free compost, and washed, lime-free grit for extra drainage; use a largish pot as it will retain the moist conditions better. Moisten the compost with boiled rainwater; this might sound a lot of trouble, but sterile conditions are important for any seed that takes time to germinate. Sprinkle the seed on the surface of the compost, and give it a light spray with some of the boiled rainwater containing fungicide, in case the seeds themselves have been in contact with any fungal disease. Cover with clingfilm or glass, and place the pot outside, in a situation out of the sun; a north-facing wall is ideal. The pot can be placed in a cold frame or plunged in ashes, and should then be left for the winter to endure the elements, as most hardy plants germinate better in the spring after a cold spell, and heather is no exception. The pots must always be moist, and if covered as mentioned and plunged to their rims, then ideal conditions will help to prevent the pots drying out.

In the spring the pots can be brought into the greenhouse or propagator to germinate at a low temperature, 7–10°C (45–50°F) keeping the compost moist and any seedlings out of the sun. Harden them off before they are placed outside to mature. Always treat them hardy, even the seedlings: there is nothing worse than weak, spindly seedlings.

When they are large enough to handle, pot them on singly in new compost, the same as before, and grow them on in dappled shade, out of strong sun, to help them to become established. These seedlings can be grown on to be planted in a specially prepared

Young seedlings just showing their colour.

Young plants showing their lovely colour.

bed – but don't forget the soil must be lime-free, unless lime tolerant plants are grown, or they will all suffer and maybe die.

Growing them on like this gives them a chance to show any qualities they possess. Many will be useless, some will be interesting, and hopefully a winner will be amongst them; but these are the F1 generation, and nothing too spectacular can be expected. The most interesting results will come from the F2 generation, which is achieved by letting the seedlings self-pollinate, or by back-crossing the best seedling to the best parent, or even to a sister seedling. All these methods bring out the recessive genes to create something new, and possibly your very own special plant.

If you want to encourage self-pollination to create the F2 or even the F3 generation, go round

tapping the stem of the flowers, as with tomato plants; however, don't do this if you are crossing with another plant, as this tapping shakes the pollen in the flower onto its own stigma, thus encouraging self-fertilization.

Grow the plants hardy, using very little in the way of fertilizers – and if you decide to use one, make sure it is high in potash so the plants will stay hard and tough to stand the winters. Water once at the beginning of the summer with sequestrene to supply the needed minerals to assure good growth and to help release the minerals that may be locked in the acid soil.

A final reminder: do not water any heathers with tapwater at any time, as most contain lime. Use only rainwater, and good results will be assured. Avoid using the hosepipe on the heather bed.

Irises

Measure of difficulty	Crossing stage	Flower to seed	Seed germination	Seedling stage
EXPERIENCE	EASY	EASY	EXPERIENCE	EASY

SITES FOR BEST RESULTS Open position; must have sunshine on the surface rhizomes to produce next year's flowers.
SPECIAL NOTES Providing the rhizomes are split after three years and kept open to the elements, many years of beautiful flowers can be expected.

The iris has never held a high position in the plant world, but it never fails to give a wonderful display, no matter how much it is neglected. It has had a long line of ancestors dating back beyond the Ancient Egyptian period, and it is because it multiplies with such ease that it has managed to survive some periods of considerable neglect. The bearded iris for instance was usually blue in colour in different variations as were most of the species irises and was referred to as the flag iris; it was generally regarded as the plant to fill a spare corner. Today, with the assistance of the plant breeder, plants of many colours and of greater size are bringing the iris to the forefront of the flower world.

The species that once sported only blue blends of colour now has many, which has encouraged a greater following. As with the bearded and the beardless iris, the flower has developed a better shape, stronger stems, and high quality, more colourful blooms with tougher petals to withstand the winds and rains that at one time would cause them to succumb.

This plant asks very little, repaying many times over even minimal care. Give it a sunny site with a well drained loam and an occasional feed, and it will reward you handsomely with a wonderful display second to none. The glorious array of colours now on offer makes it one of the most colourful on the market, and each year it will double your stock, free of charge. The full range of colour and style of flower is truly remarkable: there is the bearded range of tall,

intermediate and dwarf varieties, with hundreds of variations in each section, all with rhizome root systems. Then the beardless species incorporate not only the rhizome-rooted, but also the bulbous types which, although confusing at first, give a wide selection with which to make a start. The majority of the above species have similar sexual organ arrangements, and can be dealt with in the same manner as the tall bearded type, discussed below.

PARENT SELECTION

In the following discussion of the crossbreeding of this genus we have used as an example the tall bearded iris; however, this same method can be applied to any species of the iris family.

As usual, choosing good quality parents is essential: it is better to go to a specialist to buy two top quality plants, than trying to cross mediocre stock. This will almost guarantee top quality seedlings, providing no two detrimental traits are evident in both. If the parent plants can be seen in full flower the make-up of both their blooms can be compared, and their quality assessed: standards wide and high, just touching at the top centre, with substance and not papery, which would fold in the rain; the falls showing good width and texture, enhancing the balance of the bloom, and with a colourful beard. Side branches should be a balanced length and nicely spaced, holding the blooms clear of the stem.

THE CROSS

Before proceeding to the actual method of cross-pollination, an examination of an open flower will perhaps be helpful. The most intricate parts of the iris's sex organs are unlike normal stigmas: instead of the usual stigma, the iris has a crest or style arm with a lip or flap across the style arm; this is usually close to the crest, but it folds open to form a ledge when ripening, preparing for pollination. Before the stigma ripens the stamens can be removed, and pollen from the other flower in the cross can be applied as soon as the stigma ledge opens and becomes sticky. A stamen taken from the pollen flower can then be gently drawn along the ledge; make sure that pollen adheres – this can be seen quite easily with the naked eye, though a magnifying glass will confirm a successful operation. A paper bag can be put over the flower to prevent contamination.

Take note of the flowers not treated – a very high percentage will still be seedless, though sometimes an insect will spoil your plans. If the lower falls are taken off, it will leave insects with no landing platform. Before leaving the plant after pollination, place a label with the parentage and date of the cross for the record book. I usually pollinate all three stigmas on the plant with the same cross so that only one label need be applied, saving confusion. It is possible to pollinate each of the three stigmas with pollen from three different pollen parents;

ABOVE: *Iris showing the stigma and stamens.*

Showing the yellow stamen with the stigma crest above.

if this method is used, make sure that each one is labelled as it is crossed, otherwise the pedigree data will be lost.

THE SEED

The seedpod will soon show signs of success in the cross, and will develop to a lovely plump ovary (seed container). The seed will be ripe in about eleven to twelve weeks, according to the type of iris and the weather conditions – naturally a hot summer will ripen the seed to perfection in a shorter time. Wait for the pods to ripen: they will first turn brown at the tip and show signs of splitting open. I cut the pods a little before this happens to guarantee no loss of seed, and they can then be placed in a paper bag to ripen fully.

When the seed is completely ripe, soak them in mild diluted bleach water for two hours, then in warm water for two days, changing the water when you remember. After this period, peel away the brown coating and wash clean. Wrap the seed in wet kitchen paper towelling, then put them into a plastic bag, add the pedigree label and place in the bottom of the refrigerator for at least six weeks; plant out in pots, keeping these well watered. If placed in a warm position germination will be imminent – the iris is a hardy plant – but protect the seedlings if germinating in the warm, then harden the plants ready to be planted out in the spring. After a summer's growth the seedlings will be able to withstand the following winter with no problems.

As an alternative to the above method, the seeds can be sown in good prepared ground as soon as they are ripe, with some sharp sand in the drill to a depth of 2.5cm (1in). From late February to March some seedlings will appear, and will continue to do so spasmodically, with some waiting until the following year to make an appearance. Nevertheless the seedlings can be transplanted when around 10–15cm (4–6in) high, if growth is good, and some will even flower the following year.

When transplanting the seedlings, do not plant too deep. This can be overdone, because some seedlings are top heavy and really need a very small cane to keep them upright. Always try to cover the roots, but keep the leaves from ground level: they are

Brush pointing to crest (stigma). The stamen stands below.

Brush pointing to the stamen. The crest above is the stigma.

Iris seedlings ready for potting on.

always floppy at this early stage, and if left without support the top of the plant would probably snap off. An easier way is to leave the young seedlings together in the pot they germinated in until they are large and strong enough to stand erect on their own.

SEEDLING SELECTION

When at last the first flowers appear you can start the selection process – the seedlings will all be different, although there will be some similarities, and surprises too, no doubt; however the majority will betray faults that were not evident in the parents, but are throwbacks. These must be culled, leaving only quality plants possessing all attributes, and hopefully some extra quality features not apparent in the parents. The clever breeder will note the features required to pass on to the next generation, and will pair, say, two sister seedlings that possess the same added extra, or indeed have different extras to blend into the next line; step by step he will work to add quality at every stage, but keeping a watchful eye for any defects or deficiencies that sometimes pop up unexpectedly, and which to remedy, may require going back a generation and tracking in a different direction.

Can one of the parents add more to a quality seedling by back-crossing in the hope of strengthening already existing features? All avenues have to be studied, and thorough examination of the stock will indicate the direction to travel. Planning the next cross will be assisted by studying the records and pedigrees of the seedlings, and the more in-depth the information the more reliable will be the outcome, realizing that certain features must have come via this line or that one. Obviously, things don't always turn out the way we plan, but a planned method of approach will secure better long-term results. For instance, a fault may show in the line, one which appeared generations back and can be tracked to the culprit through the pedigree, thus showing the next step to take.

When the second or third generation have been taken using the same stock line, the plants will be showing a similarity to each other and will reflect the quality of the planning put into the crosses selected. Well thought out crosses will be reflected in the quality of the offspring, and a good planner is usually a successful breeder. When using hybrids for the first time, unexpected results will occur until a much closer pedigree is worked on, and then the family likeness will show through to create the wonderful plants we are aiming for.

Lilies

Measure of difficulty	Crossing stage	Flower to seed	Seed germination	Seedling stage
FAIRLY EASY	VERY EASY	EASY	EXPERIENCE	EASY

SITES FOR BEST RESULTS Borders, any open ground, will tolerate dappled shade, loves full sun. Slugs and snails can spoil emerging shoots. Well drained ground.

SPECIAL NOTES Split the bulbs if they get too congested. Sow the young cormlets from the main bunch to grow identical plants.

The family of the lily is a large and varied species with almost every combination of colours and patterns; with the hybrids descended from these, it provides a wonderful collection of foundation stock with which the breeder can produce more eye-catching seedlings. There are fewer than a hundred known species, but from these have come many hundreds of hybrids, some with colour combinations much better than their forefathers.

The species are growing in the wild, in natural conditions, all across the northern hemisphere, from North America, Europe and across Asia, Japan and China. Although hot, tropical conditions are not their ideal, they can be found in hot countries too, India for instance, though always up in the high, cooler regions of the mountains. The lily family has been in the limelight for many centuries, and has been depicted in drawings and mentioned

Regale lily. It is easy to grow from seed.

The lily and many other open-type flowers.

this view covers
many open-type
flowers

young seedpod at
an early stage of
development

final stages of the
seedpod before
harvesting

*Ideal plants to be used as
parents.*

in writings as far back as records go. Indeed, the first records of medieval times contain reference to *Lilium candidum*, the Madonna lily, which appears in many paintings of the past, especially within a religious context. Other species arrived in this country in the late sixteenth century, the main varieties being *L. martagon* and *L. chalcedonicum*. There was the occasional variety or two added to the collection over the years, but none produced a stir until the arrival of the first *L. regale*. This quickly became the favourite, and encouraged more interest in the growing of this wonderful species.

Over the years since their introduction into this country, many hybrids have been created which have enveloped many rewarding features, giving a variety of mixed parentage capable of creating many wonderful new hybrids of outstanding quality.

PARENTAGE SELECTION

As usual we come to the importance of selecting the very best-looking plants to carry the seedlings of future generations. All plants have certain faults and the first priority is to select two with good qualities in most departments. Once the parents have passed their 'fitness test' the hybridizing procedure can begin. One of the great benefits gained from raising plants from lily seed is the freedom from disease; and even if the parent is attacked by a virus, the seedlings are born virus free – though naturally, if left exposed to the virus, they too, will succumb.

When selection must be made on which type to transform, the varieties are endless, the choices infinite. But whatever your decision, it is certain that some improvement can be aimed for. Limit the first crosses to a select few to begin with, since each successful cross can easily provide one hundred seeds, and if you are lucky enough to rear them all, problems may arise in finding space for them. If only a few plants are to be crossed, then the procedure would be best carried out in a greenhouse; and when the flowers are ready to open on the plant growing outside, this can be taken indoors for a couple of days if no greenhouse is available. This would protect it from rain, wind and also the insects; if crossed on a lovely sunny day, then of course no problem will arise. There is never too

much trouble if the crosses are executed outside, but a cover such as a paper bag is needed to protect from intrusion and to give full confidence of purity. If the petals and stamens are removed first, then there is nothing left to attract attention.

THE CROSS

Taking the seed parent first, wait until a flower bud is about to break open; cut off the stamens straightaway, before they mature to release ripe pollen (these can be placed on a saucer where they will continue to mature to supply pollen for another cross). This leaves the stigma alone in the flower head. At this point the stigma is also immature, and can be left for a couple of days to ripen. It might be a good idea to tie a paper bag over the naked stigma; when its tip glistens with its sugary solution, it is time to apply ripe pollen from the other selected parent. Give a good coating of pollen to all the three lobes to complete the cross. The pollen is best applied by taking a ripe stamen from the other flower to the stigma, and stroking the pollen onto the three lobes. The seedpod will eventually swell, indicating that all is well, and should progress naturally unless there is adverse weather and prolonged rain: damp seedpods tend to be affected by botrytis, and it is wise to spray them with a systemic fungicide if the problem appears imminent.

Gathering the seed is really no trouble: the stem should be cut when the top of the pod goes brown and a slight slit appears as the pod starts to open; then the complete seedhead should be placed in a bag where you can shake out the seeds. There could be up to a hundred, although on close inspection many will be empty and looking like cornflakes. When they are dried the empty ones can be blown away like chaff from corn, whereas the viable ones will be more solid and easily recognized. Dry them off well before putting them away, otherwise botrytis may attack them, making them useless. Place them in a paper bag containing a seed dressing, and give them a good shake – this will be enough to protect them from harm.

On rare occasions a plant will appear to set seed and produce a very pregnant-looking pod, but on opening it there are nothing but empty seed husks

The ideal bud to emasculate.

Bud open to show the stigma and stamens.

The bud opened, stigma high in the bud. Stamens are immature ready to be cut out.

ABOVE LEFT: *Stigma ready to pollinate; the stamens are removed.*

ABOVE: *Ripe seedpods opened to reveal seeds ready to sow.*

LEFT: *Healthy seed pod, full of seed.*

that can all be blown away in the wind. Fortunately, this doesn't happen very often, and generally if a pod is green and healthy and developing after the flower has faded then good results can be expected. If a pod has developed normally, yet there appears to be nothing in it when opened, nevertheless examine the seeds thoroughly because there may be just one good seed. Nature is not so foolish as to allow the plant to continue to supply food to a pod unless there is something in it to nourish; if there are no viable seeds in the pod, then the plant stops feeding.

GROWING THE SEED

Once the seeds are dried out and in a clean condition they can be saved for sowing in the spring, or they can be sown immediately. If you intend to wait until the spring, then coat the seeds with a seed-dressing powder by placing them in a paper bag and shaking them up together; when coated they can be saved in a sealed container and kept in a cold, but not frozen, condition until required. I have had good results from seed kept for two years, although I have only tried it once.

There are so many varieties with different methods of germinating their seeds, that to start with we will use just one method that gives a generally good level of success. When experience is gained, all the ways to germinate can be used, to achieve a higher percentage of success. Some seeds germinate quickly, by sending up leaves within a few weeks; grow these on until the autumn, when the leaves die back to help build up the bulb for the following season's growth. If the later flowering varieties produce seed well into autumn, then it would be wise to sow them early the following season, giving them the full year to build the bulb to see them through the winter.

One of the most successful methods is to sow the seeds as soon as they have been cleaned. First, place them in a sieve and run water from the tap over them for a few minutes; this is because when they dry hard and ripen, they develop an inhibitor which stops them germinating until they have endured the cold and wet of a whole winter, and washing them washes away any inhibitor, as would the winter rain, and promotes quick germination. Next, almost fill the container with well drained, good seed compost,

level the surface, and then place the seed with its own space on the surface (the seed is the right size to do this); spray with a liquid fungicide such as Nimrod T, then sieve another layer of compost to cover the seed, and spray again.

The seed produced will come under a different classification depending on the variety of lily used in the cross; thus some come under the classification hypogeal immediate, others are known as hypogeal delayed; or they may be epigeal immediate, or epigeal delayed – but even though this may sound confusing, they can all be planted as the method above. It is a method of germination that dictates the classification: thus, 'epigeal' for 'above ground germination' and 'hypogeal' meaning 'underground germination'. The above ground ones (epigeal) send up their first flag leaf quickly, followed soon after by the true broad leaves; whereas the underground ones (hypogeal) germinate below ground, sending up their leaves only when a small bulb is formed. They all produce the lily seedlings we are aiming for, but it is important to understand the procedure, because it could prevent pots of underground seedling bulbs being thrown away because nothing appeared on the surface.

When the seedlings finally send up the first flag, this is quickly followed by the true leaves which are broader and are the beginning of the growth of the plant. From this time on the seedlings can be given a liquid feed, which helps to build up a strong constitution to nourish the new bulblet being formed underground. As autumn approaches the leaves

Seeds germinating in plastic bags in a cold fridge.

Potted seeds growing on.

may turn yellow as the sap flows back to the bulb, building to prepare for the winter ahead. It is important to realize that the delayed type of seed may not show any greenery for the first season, as it places all its energy into developing a fine bulb; the beginner to breeding might well think that his seeds are useless, and dispose of perfectly good miniature bulbs.

A method that is most successful for the delayed type of seed is first, to place it in a plastic bag or glass jar mixed with a good handful of damp perlite or vermiculite. The bag or jar is then sealed, labelled, and placed in a warm position for at least ten weeks; the warmth during this time should be a steady 20°C (68°F), and a kitchen is usually a good enough place, though a propagator would be much better as the temperature could then be kept constant. After this period tiny bulbs will be seen in the container. If the bulbs are as expected, they can be sown in good potting compost and placed in a cold position such as a cold frame. Providing they get a few weeks of cold, but not freezing, conditions, they will develop their true leaves as soon as the warm weather of spring stirs them into life. Without this warm, then cold, then warm again treatment, germination may take two years. If the seeds are sown in a large enough pot they can be left there until the leaves die down in the autumn; then the bulbs may be separated and replanted in

the spring, either singly in another pot or even in the nursery bed to complete their development.

If any of the new plants come up to your expectations, they can be left in their flowering positions where they will naturally develop new bulblets, all of which will produce flowers identical to the mother plant's; or they can be dug up in the autumn after the leaves have died down and divided.

Many more interesting crosses can be made by the usual crossing back to the best of the parents, though this time more exciting seedlings can be expected to appear, as this cross, the F2, is the one to supply the surprises.

Your favourite lily can be multiplied by taking off all the bulblets from the main plant, and growing them on to supply plenty of young plants for neighbours and friends. Although the choice of types to cross is a personal one, take a good overall look at what is available; plants from different parts of the world, of various forms, and from earlier varieties, including the tall, the intermediate, and now the quickly expanding population of dwarf varieties. When experience is gained, try to cross the ones that look impossible or not so obvious; if you travel up the same road as others before you, you can only expect the same achievements. Better to travel the road that no-one else has tried, and if something is found, it is usually something special.

Lupins

SIMPLICITY GUIDE

Measure of difficulty	Crossing stage	Flower to seed	Seed germination	Seedling stage
EXPERIENCE	DIFFICULT	EASY	FAIRLY EASY	EASY

SITES FOR BEST RESULTS This will tolerate most positions. Likes alkaline to neutral soil; does not grow well on acid soil.
SPECIAL NOTES Take cuttings to increase the same variety. Limit the stems to four to create the best flowers.

Lupins in a border or massed in a bed make a glorious sight, and better still when you have bred all the blooms yourself. The beds can be replenished with new and better quality varieties as they are developed and improved upon by using the very best of the new seedlings produced. An endless array of colours can be procured once a foundation stock has been established, and only top class plants will emerge when all the deficiencies are eradicated. Discard any plants that are not up to standard, and eventually the type of plant you are selectively breeding for will show through the whole stock: this will be your own strain of plants, each showing the stamp of quality you have created.

There are many species of lupin (*Lupinus*), ranging from the annual type, sometimes used by farmers to plough into the ground as a green manure, through to the tree lupin that grows as high as 1.5m (5ft), with its arching branches of small, fragrant flowers. It was in fact this tree, lupin *L. arboreus*, that was first crossed with the North American herbaceous *L. polyphyllus* by James Kelway, and which introduced a pink flower. Later, by using this variation Mr George Russell hybridized with many other combinations to produce his very famous Russell lupin strain, noted for its wonderful unprecedented array of colours.

It was quite noticeable that there was a deterioration in the quality of the strain when no particular effort was made to produce top class specimens. Without the selection of the finest and the elimination of the inferior, the downward trend was inevitable. Fortunately this came to the notice of several plant breeders who took the class in hand, with the result that more wonderful varieties are now coming onto the market. Also the lupin responds readily to good care and attention, it grows well in most soils, does not need heavy feeding, and will withstand periods of drought quite well; so if conditions are favourable, it will naturally show off in abundance.

PARENT SELECTION

If we want top quality seedlings, the parents must be of good foundation stock, and the breeder should be looking to improve on the ones available – the objective should be to create better seedlings, which in turn will become the foundation stock of the future. Healthy plants are essential, with stocky, solid, windproof spires. Do not start with flimsy spires, where the individual florets are wide apart: the spire of quality will be tight with florets, no background should be seen between each one, and they should spiral to the top still tight right to the tip. Colours should be of striking boldness, or a contrast that is clean and clear. All these are attainable as long as the breeder has an eye for blending the qualities required to mould the special characteristics that are in the genes of the selected parents, and also in the seedlings as each generation adds to the genetic bank. In fact after only two generations the type or ideal that you are aiming for will be evident, even if only to a slight degree – the important thing is to study each plant carefully, with a keen eye looking for the characteristics needed – and so a model will be created.

THE CROSS

Crossing the lupin is an easy task, though if attempted in the garden the bee can sometimes call at the wrong time, or may try to interfere with what you have in mind. It can be done, but you will need to take a few precautions. To make the task a little easier, take the plant indoors or into the greenhouse; this should guarantee the results you want, plus you will have a better percentage of seeds produced by your selected crosses. If crossing is done outdoors, then take something to sit on – you will concentrate better on your lupin spire when you are comfortable.

then remove the pollen stamens whilst they are immature, leaving the stigma that lies along the keel, like the sweet pea – this will be dealt with another day. If this procedure is being undertaken outside, then the naked stigma must be protected from the attentions of the bee or other insects. Any covering placed on the floret itself will break it off, but drive in a cane by the side of the plant so that it is a little higher than the spike, and drape a net over the whole – cane and plant – will keep things safe for a couple of days. By that time the stigma will be ripe to accept the pollen from the other selected parent. Apply the pollen with a finger or a small brush: hold a fingertip at the end of the keel, pressing it back, and the pollen will come to rest on the fingertip; it can then be carefully applied to the ripe stigma. The stigma itself is situated almost at the tip of the hard miniature seedpod, and was the same instrument that

FAR LEFT: *Petals removed from floret showing the stigma and stamens.*

LEFT: *Stigma exposed.*

BELOW: *By lightly pressing down on the petals, the pollen pops out of the tip.*

Practise first on the open florets at the base of the spike. To gather ripe pollen, hold the floret in the left hand from the back: take hold of the keel (the base) and slide it back towards the stem of the plant; this will propel the yellow pollen into your hand. This will in effect mean that the floret is now self-pollinated, as a cross, and is useless to you – but it does show how to obtain pollen from another flower when required.

Wash off the pollen from your hands before touching another floret. Try florets higher up the spike, until you open one without ripe pollen showing;

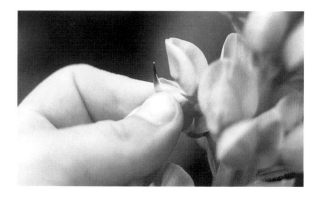

pushed the pollen onto your finger on the other plant, though in the process it was being self-pollinated. If the plant is covered for another day, a good take can be expected, as will no doubt be indicated by the swelling of the seedpod after a few days.

IN THE GREENHOUSE

If the cross is attempted in a greenhouse or indoors, then there will be no need to cover the stigma. It is possible to cross many florets on the same spike, as long as each cross is recorded as completed. If many crosses are made with the same parents on the same plant, then only one label will be required; but if there are mixed crosses on the same plant, tie a slip of coloured cotton onto each crossed floret, a different colour for each cross, and record the colour to the parentage of the cross. Always remember that the florets are very delicate and are snapped off easily, so take extra care.

SOWING THE SEED

The seedpods will be fattening as the summer gets hotter, and usually there is no trouble ripening them; when the dark green pods look dry and ready to break open, they should be harvested – and don't forget them or your seeds will scatter all over the place. Rather, pick a little early and place them in a paper bag to ripen off, keeping the bag closed to prevent any seed flying out as the pod pops open. The seed can be kept until the spring, or sown as soon as it is ripe; by sowing immediately, the seed is up before the winter sets in, and if given slight cover during the winter a very early start is made in the spring – so you will have a spike to show you what has been produced the very next season. Naturally this one will lack the strength of the one in the following season, but a fair assessment can be made as to its quality: thus a good thick spike on a seedling will augur well for the following year, as well as show the colour to be expected.

If only a few plants are required, then sow the seed singly in pots in a warm place to germinate quickly; these will have developed nicely by the time winter approaches. The seedlings would probably survive a

More successful crossings, promising seed. The pods are developing.

winter in the open, but it is safer to place them for the cold period in a frame, where they will have developed a good root system by the spring. As the weather becomes warmer the young plants can be planted out in good ground; water them well, and the root system developed during the cold season will give them a marvellous start.

If a spring sowing is preferred, then the plants will be that much later – they could produce a small spike by late summer. However, they will be well established by the winter, and can stay in their permanent planted position. A good seed compost is ideal for lupin seed, as long as extra drainage is organized – most of all the plant hates wet conditions. The lupin is very hardy and will withstand frosts, but as a seedling it is better to start it inside in the conditions suggested where progress can be made, rather than have it remain dormant until the warmer weather approaches.

SEEDLING SELECTION

When the seedlings are in full bloom the comparison between them and their parents will indicate any progress – though at this stage very little change is likely because these are the F1 hybrid and the dominant colour usually overrides any other. The quality in other departments may be seen, however, and the poor specimens will be well to the fore – which is why a self-cross to produce the F2 generation is advised, or a back-cross to the best parent, or even to a good sister seedling; but don't bring in any more outcrosses at this time.

Any plants showing poor qualities should be removed immediately, as they will only pass on the unfavourable characteristics. Keep detailed records of all the crosses made, and a pattern will soon emerge showing the best direction in which to progress to achieve the type of plant required.

BETTER TYPES

A plant with erect, stately spikes with a dense, compact floret formation is always an impressive sight. Choice of colour is more personal, and everyone has his own favourite; but whatever it may be, the breeder will be aiming for a single colour that is strong and vibrant, or a pastel shade with a delicate look but on a vigorous stem. Once this standard is reached, selective progressive crossing will produce truly wonderful blooms, an achievement that will bring enormous pleasure – as I have experienced myself, in particular when I produced a very dark maroon of outstanding quality with a very dense, tight spike with hundreds of florets, every one touching its neighbour, and standing like a cathedral spire.

THE BEST FROM THE BEST

When growing mature plants, whether in singles or groups, the finest blooms are achieved by limiting the spikes to four for each plant, cutting out any others and using them as cutting material, or discarding. This method keeps plants healthier and more robust for longer, and produces the best quality blooms.

Once a particular favourite has arrived it is natural to want to increase the number of identical plants, and the only way to achieve this is to split the main plant or to take cuttings. The split can be made in the autumn or in the early spring, and the cleaner the cut, the quicker the scar will heal. A word of warning here: this is when a virus or other disease can start to rot off the whole root, a situation that can be avoided, or the chances of it happening at least reduced, by dipping the cut pieces into a fungicidal mixture for a few minutes.

After a few seasons of perfecting the type of plant you favour, it will be apparent that the strain you have created runs though all your stock; and if a certain deviation has been administered, this will show up in every seedling until other characteristics are used to modify the structure.

Seedlings on trial.

Pansies and Violas

Measure of difficulty	Crossing stage	Flower to seed	Seed germination	Seedling stage
FAIRLY EASY	TRICKY TO PERFECT	EASY	EASY	EASY

SITES FOR BEST RESULTS This genus will grow almost anywhere in well drained soil. It will take full sun or part shade, and if dead-headed it will flower the whole season.

SPECIAL NOTES If sprayed with fungicide and insecticide it will grow to perfection, giving a wonderful display.

Many people have a soft spot in their hearts for pansies and violas, mainly perhaps because these small, tender-looking plants show a particular toughness against the worst weather. They have also survived many hundreds of years, sketches and drawings from way back proving that they were in existence long ago. All the top quality varieties today are descended from the small-flowered plants depicted by the artists of the past.

For the more botanically minded, there are over 400 species, ranging from heartsease, dog tooth violet, violetta, and many more of the viola species. These variable types must have grown almost unchanged for thousands of generations, only slight mutations changing their development over the years. Early recordings are known from prints and woodcuts, and they are also mentioned in the writings of some of our eminent poets.

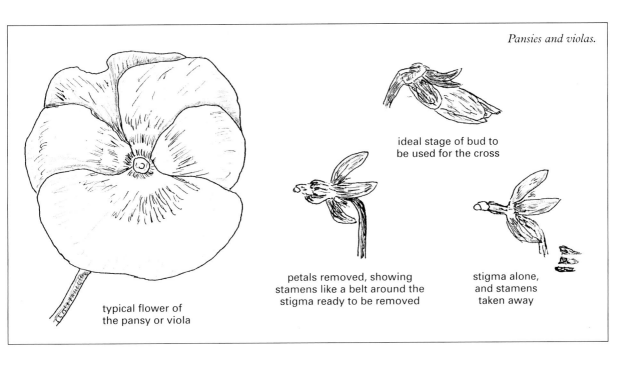

Pansies and violas.

ideal stage of bud to
be used for the cross

typical flower of
the pansy or viola

petals removed, showing
stamens like a belt around the
stigma ready to be removed

stigma alone,
and stamens
taken away

Improvements in the species, particularly concerning the pansy and the viola, did not occur until the early 1800s, but since then many new varieties have appeared – indeed, there are so many today that rather than name each individual, they are now classed separately as strains, which includes many colours and variations from the same family.

In recent years many special varieties have been given names by breeders who have stabilized the flower – or 'fixed it' as they say – by interbreeding, so that each flower possesses the same gene structure. This chapter describes this procedure.

THE BEE AT WORK

The flower is self-fertile, meaning that each flower can be pollinated by its own pollen. However, nature has also equipped it with an ingenious mechanism that favours outcrossing. Study of the flower will reveal that the lower petal is the landing platform for bees; the centre of the flower is bright yellow, with guidelines to show where the nectar lies: this is contained at the base of the spur at the back of the flower in the shape of a tube made by the continuation of the broad landing petal. In order to reach this nectar, the bee has to push past the stigma, a small mouthpart shaped like a cup with a lower lip, and in doing so, scrapes off into the cup the pollen from other flowers already on its head.

Furthermore, during its foraging for the nectar, the five stamens that are laid all round the stigma like a belt, are disturbed, with the result that pollen is dislodged and adheres to the head of the bee, ready to pollinate another flower. On retreating out of the flower, gathering more pollen, the bee has to pass the stigma cup, and as it does so, the lip of the stigma is pushed up, so covering the 'mouth' and preventing its own pollen from self-pollinating: nature's ingenious way of discouraging inbreeding on this particular species.

The flower is quite fertile for several days. Of the five stamens, the top one releases pollen first, dropping it onto the hairs of the bottom and side petals. Two days later two more stamens release pollen, and two days after that, the last two surrender their golden grains. Each flower is in a pollinating state for quite a few days.

BREEDING

Pansies and violas have been hybridized so many times that the genes of every plant have so many variations as to make it almost impossible to predict the outcome of a cross. It is generally agreed that the way to multiply a particular seedling with the characteristics preferred is by splitting the plant; this is not so easy with the pansy, but the viola is a more obliging subject. Pansies usually have one main stem at the root, spreading from about ground level, and this makes any splitting up of the plant difficult, and sometimes impossible. Cuttings are the most favourable option, which is why most pansies are grown from seed. The viola is an easier plant as regards vegetative multiplication; cuttings can be established, but the viola's main attribute is having a root system that can be quite readily split apart, so more plants of the same clone are easily obtained.

After considering the methods of pollination by the insect world, it will be appreciated that in order to procure a perfect cross from our selected plants, it is essential to isolate them. The plant selected as the seed bearer can be placed in a greenhouse or even on a window ledge, away from the bee; moreover if the plants were kept isolated like this they would not set seed because nature would class them as preferred outbreeders. Isolation assists the breeding programme because you don't have to emasculate the flower: just apply your own selected pollen to the cup of the stigma.

A small artist's paint brush is all that is required for this operation: take hold of the first flower to open, one hand holding the back of the flower on the stem, the other taking hold of the base petal, pulling down gently to 'snap' the petal. This does not mean pulling it off, but keeping it in a low position so as to allow clear access to the stigma, and also to prevent any pollen from this flower contacting its own stigma. This prepares the seed parent; so now to the pollen plant. In fact there is no preparation required of the pollen plant other than locating the presence of ripe pollen, and having it positioned in close proximity for convenience.

To make the first cross, place the bristles of the brush into the centre of the flower of the intended male bloom, preferably to one side, at the same

Unnamed new variety.

The ideal bud to emasculate ready to cross-pollinate.

Petals and stamens removed ready for pollen.

time twirling the brush between the fingers: this action brings the bristles together almost to a point. Slowly sweep the brush under the stigma to the other side; on withdrawing it you will notice the almost white pollen on the tip of the brush. This is then applied to the cup at the tip of the stigma of the seed plant.

When a plant is producing many flowers, this procedure can continue every day to all the flowers. Make sure that all the flowers are pollinated every day until you see the collapse of the petals. By this time it will be very noticeable that the ovule (seedpod) has started swelling, a sure sign of a successful fertilization. If several plants are to be pollinated, the best and most foolproof method is to use one brush for one plant's pollen; then stick the brush into the pot, the bristles uppermost – thus the following day the correct brush is on hand, with no fear of mixing the pollen from another plant. This practice is better than sterilizing in methylated spirits or alcohol for every cross; having several brushes is not too expensive, and if looked after they will last a lifetime. Squirrel, sable or camel hair brushes are perfect; nylon is almost useless. Buy good artists' brushes with very few bristles: these are definitely to be preferred to bushy ones.

As the seedpods swell, the plants can be placed outside to mature, though keep a watchful eye on the ripening process: if left too long the pod will open, exposing the seed to the elements, and if left

Seed pods ripening.

BELOW: *Ripe seeds ready for harvesting.*

even longer, the three parts of the seedpod will dry, contract, and shoot off the seed in all directions. If the tips of the pods are becoming dry, and the pod fully swollen, then the pod can be cut off and placed in a closed paper bag: as the pod opens and dries, the seeds will shoot out of the pod, but will be safely retained in the bag. The seed will be a lovely golden brown colour.

SEED SOWING

Experience has shown that to sow the seed as soon as it is ripe gives almost 100 per cent germination. If, on the other hand, the seed is to be kept for spring sowing, it is essential to first dry, then seal the seed carefully in an airtight container. If left to overwinter in a paper bag for instance, the return will be less than 50 per cent – very little for the work involved.

If pansy and viola seed is sown as soon as it is ripe, the returns are impressive. Using the best seed compost, lightly press down to level the surface of the soil, then water well before sowing the seed onto the surface. Lightly press the seed into the surface to create good contact with the soil, then either give a very light sprinkle of soil, or not at all: both methods work. Then cover with clingfilm to keep the surface of the soil moist. Next, place the seed trays in a dark position, or cover with a dark material, for

instance a piece of the compost bag cut with scissors to the right size. Examine in a few days and uncover as soon as the seeds germinate, bringing them into the light, but avoiding bright sunshine.

It is advisable to germinate the seed at 23°C (73°F) or a little above; this has proved very successful, with the first seedlings appearing between fourteen and twenty-one days. If notes are kept, it will be found that the brighter coloured plants are the first to appear, with the ones in the paler colour range being slower to germinate: this seems to be true of most plants.

The F1 generation will consist of an abundance of seedlings and many variations, mainly because so many hybrid genes are present in all the modern varieties. Certain factors will no doubt have shown themselves, whether complementary attributes or unwanted weaknesses, but at this stage this is to be expected.

SEEDLING SELECTION

Growing on the seedlings to their first flowering will result in terrific variation, and a beginner might wonder where he went wrong in his quest for his ideal plant. But good results will soon follow.

Select the seedlings nearest to the ideal from the first F1 hybrid batch; when in flower, these can be crossed back again to the best parent, producing seedlings containing 75 per cent of the first parent's genes. This cross will result in a closer knit family of seedlings with less variety and a more pronounced

ABOVE: *Prize winning blooms.*

family likeness, whether of the colour or type of plant. If from the F2 generation an ideal can be selected, the next step is to self-cross the ideal by applying its own pollen to its own stigma, again keeping the plant isolated. By this cross, your ideal will be more or less fixed – and provided this self-cross technique is applied, a plentiful supply of almost identical plants will be available from the seed saved.

The same method can be used by crossing two sister seedlings, to start the process of fixing the characteristics in the plants. If a certain colour needs to be retained, using the methods as above will fix the selected colour, as long as you cross back to the same family in a selective way, and only make the cross between two plants of the same colour.

SIDE-TRACKING

During this application to stabilize the family likeness, many wonderful combinations of colours will appear, as well as small and large flowers; moreover, some will perhaps be more beautiful than the intended type, adding another line to your programme. There is no reason not to start a new family line, provided this does not side-track you away from the original – or you could end up with a real mixed bag and no complete conclusion.

Healthy seedlings.

Pelargoniums (Geraniums)

Measure of difficulty	Crossing stage	Flower to seed	Seed germination	Seedling stage
FAIRLY EASY	EASY TO LEARN	EASY	EASY	EASY

SITES FOR BEST RESULTS These plants are always grown in beds and borders and these are the best places to grow them. Windowsills, the conservatory or windowboxes are fashionable.

SPECIAL NOTES Once the crossing stage is mastered, this is a very rewarding plant. Some lovely colours and leaf combinations can be achieved.

For as far back as I can remember, the pelargonium has always suffered the confusion of having two names; I grew up to know that geraniums were the red flower types whilst the multicoloured ones were pelargoniums. In fact they are all pelargoniums, and there is yet more confusion when a nurseryman insists on marking his pelargonium plants as geraniums, thereby misinforming the public. Nevertheless, whichever name is used, this is a wonderful plant, and quite capable of holding its own in the world of flowers.

The *pelargonium* has been around for a very long time and has references from India and South Africa and even Australasia: from this we see that it is a plant adapted to warmer climes, which explains the losses incurred by frost. They appear to have been grown in this country in the 1600s, and were thought to have first arrived in Europe from South Africa, India and the Far East, on the route taken by the tea clippers of the East India Company and other trading explorers. The species of that period would be far removed from today's standards, which proves the value of the crossbreeding programmes whether by the hand of man or with the assistance of insects.

Amongst enthusiasts there appears to be two camps: those who grow the tender *pelargonium*, and those who prefer the hardy *geranium* (the *cranesbill*) – and it is very unusual to find them party to the same stable. This may be because of the length of flowering time – to see a whole range of hardy *geraniums* dominating the borders is an impressive sight. Unfortunately it is so short a time – but we could say that of many of our flowering plants. An aim for our budding hybridist might be to extend the flowering period, something that was achieved with the *pelargonium* and the modern pink.

Many varieties of the hardy *geranium* have sterile flowers, usually certain hybrids that have been created from species with a different chromosome count, a stumbling block for many a proposed cross. If good records are kept of all crosses made, it will become clear which are in this category, thus saving wasted efforts in the future; but don't confuse sterility with incompatibility, otherwise a good plant may be sidelined as sterile when it would in fact be compatible to a different variety.

Much trial and error can be contemplated, and many unexpected variations will be on offer, but keeping records that may be studied at a quiet time will very often reveal the direction in which to proceed. When the seedlings from a cross mature and can be compared to the parents, an assessment can usually be made as to the qualities handed down. However, remember that although a back-cross may fix the good points, it must be fully appreciated that it will almost certainly also accentuate any detrimental characteristics apparent in both parent and seedling.

If, as is hoped, a lovely seedling appears in the F1 crop, this could be the start of a new strain from which many similar seedlings would be developed. By selfing, the seedling would not necessarily produce identical plants – they would most likely be different, but showing some similarities. However, if the two that were nearest to identical were selected from the seedlings and crossed again, then some

closer relation to identity would be imminent. Crossing the closest to identical again would in time produce almost perfect likenesses.

Unfortunately this method would lead to a loss of that hybrid vigour which is so important to the production of quality stock in the pelargonium. If two separate lines of plants, using this self-crossing method, were used until the identical lines showed finally fixed, then a hand cross made between the two lines would give the F1 hybrid which should produce seedlings with the same identity and, more important, the hybrid vigour that is paramount to the success of the strain. This method is used by the seed companies to produce the F1 hybrids that are understandably expensive to buy – but the results are worth the cost.

THE CROSS

If many crosses are on the agenda, then isolating the ones to be used will be an advantage; these can be grown in pots placed in the greenhouse or even

ABOVE: *Always use a bud as a female parent. No insect has spoiled it.*

The stamens are showing but the stigma is too young to be seen.

The stigma is showing, now the stamens are past their best.

The stigma is ready when it splits at the tip as in this picture.

BELOW: *The stigma ready to be pollinated.*

on the windowsill until after the cross has been made and the seedpods are set. This method not only makes certain the cross is the one you intended, but is convenient if the weather is bad. When the individual florets on the flower head open, the stamens can be removed before pollen is released, leaving the immature stigma; this takes a few days to develop – you will see its tip unfurling, exposing its five receptive areas which have a sticky coating to receive the pollen grains. A magnifying glass is useful, to examine the stigma after pollination to see that the pollen coating is adequate; if in doubt, add another coating. If both the stigma and the pollen grains are in peak condition, then a few hours later fertilization will have taken place and the seed will be developing to maturity.

If the plant to be crossed is in a greenhouse or indeed on a windowsill, then the stamens can be left in place, the reason being that they become ripe and shed their pollen before the stigma is ripe. As the pollen dies, the stigma becomes ripe and opens its tip, to reveal the five sticky landing pads for pollen from another floret, whether this arrives by the wind, insects or man. Obviously, in the greenhouse this does not happen unless pollination is assisted.

Don't forget to name the parents in the cross, marking the seed parent first and then the pollen parent, and keeping the tag with them throughout.

SEED HARVEST

Whilst the seed is in the developing stage the stigma grows out like a long spear; when ripe, this opens up like an umbrella with the material missing, each wire holding a seed. At this stage either cover with a bag, or collect the head to ripen it off indoors, otherwise the seeds will fall and be lost. From fertilization to maturity varies between six to eight weeks in a good summer; with hot weather some may mature in five weeks, but on average the former is the usual.

The seeds will keep well until the spring provided they are dried off well; any sign of dampness and mildew will take over. Keep them in a paper bag and no harm will come to them, as long as they are not left where frost will affect them.

SEED SOWING

The seed can be parted from the fluffy tails they were born with; this usually also takes off the unwanted husks. Using a good quality brand of seed compost, the seed can be spaced out to allow each one room to develop – the size of the seed making this task very easy – then cover with a thin layer of compost and water in well. Try to keep at a constant temperature of 21–24°C (70–75°F) until the seedlings emerge. Pot on into small pots when large enough to handle, and keep in a light position to maintain a stocky plant; then harden off before planting outside, after all the frosts are finished. When the weather is warm during the day but frosty at night, stand the seedlings in their pots outside in the sunshine to help harden them off – but don't forget to take them back under cover at night.

NEXT STAGE SELECTION

The exciting time arrives as the flower buds begin to break open. When a cross between two favourite plants has been made, the expectancy is all part of the excitement – and even if the end result is not quite what was anticipated, the plants will hopefully slot nicely into the planned breeding programme. Further crossbreeding with the best of the offspring may become a foundation for the new strain you may be in the process of developing.

Selecting the foundation stock can be quite challenging, as there are so many varieties and countless combinations and colours to whet the appetite. Many of the new varieties released today are produced by the amateur hybridist, and many more are still to be found. The ones with the pretty coloured leaves are called zonals, and these alone are worthwhile to grow, with the added attraction of some beautiful single and double flowers. Then there is the type known as 'regal', showing some very exotic colourings; and the trailing ivy-leaved and scented types – all of these give creative opportunities. It is certain that many new varieties are still locked away in Mother Nature's treasure chest. The breeder of ability can unlock these varieties and bring them onto the scene for the pleasure of all.

Phlox

Measure of difficulty	Crossing stage	Flower to seed	Seed germination	Seedling stage
DIFFICULT	NOT EASY	EASY	EASY	EASY

SITES FOR BEST RESULTS Usual position is the long border; they are good back-of-the-border plants. They will grow in any type of soil. Good feeding and fungicide spray will reap a harvest of beautiful heads of lovely colours, worth all the trouble.

SPECIAL NOTES The crossing stage has to be mastered, then results are assured. It is invaluable once perfected.

This plant appears to have lost some of the popularity it had in recent years; however, it can still hold a very important position at the centre of a herbaceous border. In the days of large country gardens, phlox were held in high esteem, and gracefully emblazoned the long avenues of perennials. Those were the days when every large country home went to great lengths to enchant their visitors with their spectacular gardens. Taking pride of place in the border, with its tall, elegant spikes – whites, blues, reds, dark mauves and every colour in between – was the proud-standing phlox. Maybe

Typical flower.

the fact that stakes were required if it was planted in a windy border contributed to its decline; nevertheless, this plant is still a stately contender to the summer collection in any garden.

The phlox genus numbers some fifty species, and was originally native to North America. Here, we are most interested in just three: first, *Phlox paniculata*, or rather its descendants, without doubt one of the showiest and most attractive border plants of them all; also *P. maculata*, a fully hardy type of similar stature, of which 'Omega' is a descendant, a lovely white with a shell-pink centre, and a wonderful starting plant. For the rockery enthusiast there are some specials, to start with *P. chatahoochee*, a red-eyed, pinky lavender showing an abundance of bloom, its only requirements being a sunny position in well drained soil.

From these individuals have derived some very spectacular varieties that dominate the borders today, with stronger stems and more robust flower heads, all coming from the blending of the selected varieties bred by the hybridist. It must be said that an eel-worm resistant variety would be a blessing to the gardener who is unfortunate to be troubled by this pest! Particular mention should be made of the gorgeous white *P. paniculata* 'Figiyama', and the bright red *P.p* 'Starfire' with its very dark foliage: these are unusual amongst the standard colour range of these plants, and give a clear idea of what a breeder can achieve in the crossing of these varieties. Naturally a purist will find other combinations to perfect the single colours, but there is a range to cover any need.

Over the years, colours have become more vivid and less wishy-washy than in the earlier varieties, giving an excellent pointer to the type of plant required in the search for perfection, namely a sturdy, strong-stemmed, medium-height specimen, capable of holding aloft the bold, multi-flowered heads. It is unfortunate that the wonderful modern heads are so large that they are almost too much for the stem to carry: if rainwater adds too much extra weight to the stem, it collapses, with disastrous results. *P. paniculata* reaches about 1.2m (4ft) in height, whereas *P. maculata* is lower, at 1m (3ft), this is helpful to know when planning their final position if they are to withstand inclement weather. The rockery types don't have this difficulty and can be grown in pots to cross-breed on the greenhouse bench. The tall ones can also be pot-grown, and can be dealt with whilst still on the ground – or the breeder could sit on a stool.

PARENT SELECTION

It takes the same amount of effort to grow a poor specimen as it does to grow a good one, so why not start with the best that can be bought? Using inferior stock plants will produce only mediocre offspring and will guarantee disappointment. Take a look at the prize plants at a flower show, and you will soon get to know the qualities required. The head, or truss as it is called, should have a balanced overall look, showing every pip (individual flower) open to perfection, with a good strong colour, solid throughout; finally it should be held proudly on the strong, stout stems.

Over a period of growing phlox, it will be noticed that certain varieties set seed without any trouble, whilst others – and these tend to be the better varieties – fail to set whatever the conditions. This is useful to know to save wasting time by trying to use this type of plant as the seed parent. Nevertheless, the poor seeder may give good fertile pollen, which is a bonus to producing plants of good flowering quality; besides, the resulting seedlings may be good seed-bearing plants themselves.

When selecting stock plants, study the plants in bloom at a nursery or garden centre: the whole constitution of the plant should be capable of standing up to bad winds and rain, so it is important to select ones that are capable of holding their own in adverse conditions; then with the right cross you should be able to produce quality seedlings that will be your stock plants of the future.

Colour is then the choice of your own preference, though some hues are more appealing to the general public than others. For shape and appearance, these are the guidelines to follow: the truss or flower head as a whole has to be as though solid, with all the pips (individual florets) just touching, making the pyramid-shaped head. The flower head begins to open at the top florets, working down the truss until all are open together – and if the florets (pips) open so that all five petals appear as a flat surface with no curled ones, the look of the truss will be excellent, and a fitting reward for good parentage selection.

MAKING THE CROSS

Now that the parents have been selected, we will first consider the seed-bearing plant. As soon as possible when the floret is just about to open, gently take off the five petals or just open them, pressing them back. Remove all the stamens before the pollen ripens. These can be placed on a saucer to ripen, and can be used to cross with another plant; this will leave the stigma alone, erect in the middle of the floret. At this stage it is too immature to receive pollen, so wait until its tip ripens – it splits into three sections and

Ideal buds to emasculate.

Upper flower bud opened, showing stigma and stamens.

Top flower has stamens removed, showing stigma.

becomes sticky with a glistening moisture. Apply the pollen from your other selected parent flower to all three sections; a magnifying glass is useful to check that a good amount has adhered to all parts. Once the stigma has received a good coating of pollen, there is no real reason to cover the head, as the honey bee seems to bypass the phlox and the bumble bee appears to attack the floret from underneath to gain access to the nectar. The usual tip: if there are several different crosses made on the same truss, mark each cross with a different coloured cotton and make a note of the details of the parentage relative to each colour on a large label tied to the main plant stem. This method is absolutely foolproof.

THE SEED

If the crosses were successful, the seed should be harvested by mid-August or September – and watch out for birds, as they sometimes like the taste of them. Collect them as they ripen until all are gathered; some pods hold up to four seeds, and many just one. Leave the pods on the plant for as long as you dare – but too long, and the pods split and the seed is scattered. If in doubt, cut off the floret on its little stem and place it in a dry box, covering it with newspaper to prevent any seed from shooting out of the box: phlox seeds tend to fly, as do pansy seeds.

SOWING THE SEED

The lifespan of the seed is all too short unless it is sealed as the seed merchants do, or placed in a sealed container and kept in a refrigerator. Alternatively, as soon as the seed has dried off thoroughly you can sow it into a tray of seed compost, place it in a cold frame which is on the shady side – and forget it, except to make sure it doesn't lack moisture.

Plant out the seedlings in the spring, in good, well prepared ground: they will grow happily, and will flower and give a fine head the first year, even though they will not reach full height until the second year. As they show off their respective beauties, it is time to assess the qualities passed down from the parents. Are they better, or as good? Are there any features that can be combined with, say, another seedling or in a back-cross to one of the parents? These are your F1 hybrids, and self-crossing the seedlings will produce your F2 generation. Using this method, and back-crossing to a good sister seedling or the better parent, will produce the family where a winner is most likely to appear.

If by any chance a beautiful seedling arrives, then dividing the plant is the best option to multiply the stock; root cuttings will also achieve the same results, and with these you have the advantage of starting with eelworm-free stock again if the parent plant becomes a victim to this disease.

Some of the modern-day plants have gone a long way to rectify the frailties of the species but more room for additional merits can and will be exploited in the future and you could be one of the explorers to achieve this.

Pinks and Carnations

SIMPLICITY GUIDE

Measure of difficulty	Crossing stage	Flower to seed	Seed germination	Seedling stage
FAIRLY EASY	FAIRLY EASY	EASY	EASY	EASY

SITES FOR BEST RESULTS Providing the ground is not acid, these plants will grow in most positions. They prefer open sunny spots, whether borders or rockeries, and well drained conditions.
SPECIAL NOTES Spray with systemic fungicide once a month and keep a watch for greenfly, and the results are guaranteed. It prefers a more alkaline soil.

Pinks and Carnations both belong to the dianthus family, which includes many species, in fact more than three hundred. We will be dealing with the modern varieties because this is definitely the way forward, although many older varieties have many attributes that could be used in building up the present-day types.

The advantages of the present-day plants over the older ones are quite outstanding; one of the most important is the continuation of flowering through the summer months instead of one flush show, also the stronger stems mean that today's flowers make ideal vase fillers as well as border classics, the continued flowering of the perpetuals giving the florist the privilege of being able to sell carnations at any time of the year. There are enormous variations in colour too, promising a range of possibilities in the breeding of new cultivars.

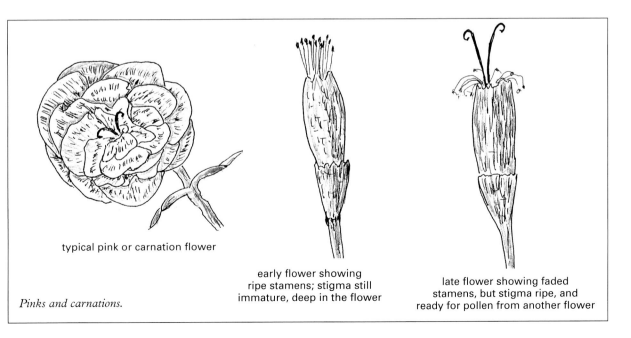

typical pink or carnation flower

early flower showing
ripe stamens; stigma still
immature, deep in the flower

late flower showing faded
stamens, but stigma ripe, and
ready for pollen from another flower

Pinks and carnations.

It is often said that perfume is lacking in present-day plants, and it is true that many new ones are disappointing in this respect; but there are modern-day plants possessing the clove scent, and the modern pinks have a wonderful variation of perfume: when all my own new varieties are in bloom in the greenhouse the scent is breathtaking, and I can guarantee that the first thing mentioned by any visitor is the perfume with remarks on the beautiful colours following later on. A wonderful example of this is 'Oakwood Crimson Clove', raised by Mr Sid Hall, who dominates the breeding and showing of pinks at the present time.

Pinks and carnations have been grown for thousands of years, and are believed to have originated from Asia and Europe. The Romans and the Greeks grew them, but like all plants at that time, they were designated for medicinal purposes; these would most likely have grown in the wild, where some were used to flavour drinks. It is said that these plants were grown mainly for their perfume, as a way of overwhelming the smells of poor sanitation.

Dianthus caryophyllus, the original carnation, was described by Theophrastus as far back as 300 BC, but that was a mere five-petalled flower. It was found at a later date around southern Europe, but its main habitat was in France, and particularly in Normandy; it was said to have been introduced into England at the time of the Norman Conquest. Since that time, many introductions of many variations of pinks and carnations have arrived on the scene from many parts of Europe and other areas around the world, all possessing slight differences, and when cross-pollinated, these all added to the genetic bank in the offspring.

All these modern hybrid varieties have such a varied genetic make-up that any cross between them would produce a very mixed family of seedlings. Many breeders cross anything that is ripe or convenient at the time, in the hope that something special will appear; this approach may produce a one-off winner, and often does, but the amount of rubbish to accompany this winner is a waste of valuable time and space. Growing a pathetic plant from seed to maturity uses the same resources as growing a quality plant, and any method that will avoid this wasted effort is worthy of consideration. Only the best plants should be included in the programme, and good records should be kept: it will be found that some

plants when crossed produce excellent seedlings, and others throw off rubbish even when crossed with a super partner. These failed parents need to be discarded and listed in the records as a failure, to prevent the same problem being repeated.

When a certain cross produces special seedlings it can be repeated, and should be considered the cornerstone of the pedigree, the one to build on. After several lines using the same quality plants in various combinations, the family resemblance will begin to take shape; some indifferent plants will also put in an appearance, but if selection is uppermost in mind, then quality will prevail. Any advancement in breeding new, improved cultivars is, as in most plant breeding, only achieved with dedication and patience, in particular when coping with disappointments.

MAKING A START

A good starting point, indeed an essential one, is to visit as many pink and carnation shows as possible. This is the best way to see at first hand the finest and latest varieties, many of which are not obtainable on the open market, but are still in the hands of the breeder and his close friends. Nevertheless, all these new plants are generally available direct from the breeder, who may be approached at the show – these showmen are always very helpful and extremely generous to newcomers. By acquiring the newest, as well as the best of the older varieties, your breeding programme will be on a par with the best of them, and all that is required now is experience.

The cuttings bought, from whatever source, will be in small pots, and the plants will be about 15cm (6in) high; they will also have had their first stop – the growing tip will have been taken out to encourage side-shoots. If this were to be left, the centre stem would grow up to flower, but it would have no side-shoots, or very few, with which to continue to produce flowers. On rare occasions this lone stem will be all that is supplied for the season.

Stopping will therefore result in a more robust plant with several stems forming, and it will soon require potting on to the next size pot. This stage will take the plant into the flowering phase in early summer, ready for assessment as to parental quality.

CROSS BREEDING

Some knowledge of the flowering strategy of the plant is essential, to know how to tackle the cross-breeding operation. As the flower opens, the stamens will soon become ripe with pollen, but only

in a plentiful supply in the single-petalled flowers. The double flowers have very little pollen, and some none at all, because they have utilized the stamens to create more petals; thus they have deprived themselves of the means with which to supply pollen. Sometimes the very small petals in the centre of the bloom will show a very small portion of the remains of the stamens, and in fact a few grains of pollen may be found there. A magnifying glass to look into the centre of any bloom will reveal pollen grains somewhere around, even if not on the stamens. However, even if this double flower is of no use for pollen, it will be ideal to use as the seed parent, the seed head will be allowed to stay on the plant when the petals die down.

As the bloom matures, its own pollen will have dried up and the stigmas will be slowly protruding from the centre. When full length, these snail-like horns will curl at the ends and be ready to receive the pollen from the selected pollen parent onto their sticky receptor pads; the pollen can be applied with a fine artist's brush or a small strip of blotting paper, a new piece for every cross.

After pollination the pollen grows down the stigma, through the style to the ovaries to fertilize the ovules, so forming the seeds. A couple of days after

ABOVE: *Showing the two white stigmas ready to be crossed.*

The three stages - stamens, stigma and seedpod.

fertilization the flower closes like an inside-out umbrella, all the petals coming together; this is a good sign of success. As the flower fades and the petals begin to shrivel, it is a wise precaution to gently tear open the calyx to expose the seedpod, carefully plucking out the old petals one by one to prevent moisture rotting them, which will undoubtedly damage the vital parts. When the crossing operation takes place in the confines of a greenhouse these precautions are not really necessary, but at the discretion of the grower – but they are always something to keep in mind.

It will be noticed that as the pollen is ripe in the flower, there is no sign of a stigma: that is because the stigmas are low down in the flower, and immature when the pollen is ripe. As the pollen dries and becomes ineffective, this triggers the growth of the stigmas, which grow out above the petals; at this stage the stigma tips will curl and become sticky, ready to receive pollen from another flower. This is nature's way of securing a cross from another flower, and is her clever technique to aid cross-pollination. To encourage pollen production in plants that are reluctant to co-operate, pick a pink flower when young, and place it in a small bottle of water in the greenhouse, in full sun; this works well on double flowers as well as the single ones.

Just as the better double blooms of pinks and carnations are ideal parent plants, it will be found that single and semi-double flowers are better for pollen-bearing, with pollen in abundance on many plants. Using this type of cross it will be found that many single and semi-double flowers will be amongst the new seedlings.

When doubles are crossed with doubles, sometimes a plant evolves with such abundance of petals that the calyx splits, making the flower useless. However, although this is a major fault, a large flower can be crossed with a single or semi-single plant, and on occasions produces beautiful, perfect double plants. When the double bloom flower is used as a seed parent, greater success will be had by using the second or third flower on the stem. Although slightly smaller, these flowers seem to be more fruitful, and their smaller size will in no way affect the size of the future seedlings from this cross. The first leading flower on the plant often tends to abort which is why the second or third flowers are used.

HARVESTING

When the seedpod shows signs of developing, it is wise to keep the pod as dry as possible, because the least water on it will quickly rot the inner part, destroying the seed. The pod swells quickly, and will reach its full size in about six weeks, when it will begin to turn brown, firstly at the tip, then progressing down the pod. When the brown reaches halfway down the pod it should be taken from the plant, to finish drying in a paper bag. Take care of the seed because they are brittle and easily split, which would make them absolutely useless; they are mostly jet black or dark brown in colour. If the seedpod is opened too early, the seed will be a cream colour and very soft, and these are often of no use; however, the firmer ones, even though still cream in colour, could produce seedlings. Nevertheless it is still a gamble, and really not worth the time and effort, unless the seeds come from a special cross. The best advice is, wait until the pod is fully ripe.

Seed can be kept in a cool dry place until the spring, but sowing immediately gives a high percentage of success because of the freshness of the seed. These seedlings will require the protection of at least a cold frame, but if there is none available, then a spring sowing is to be advised; although the seedlings are hardy, they would benefit from a slight protection from the worst of the elements.

COMPOST

Compost for seed sowing is easy to find, and all the proprietary brands will give a good start to seed germination, although it is a good idea to add extra grit or sand to aid drainage. Selecting a suitable potting-on material is more difficult, because no matter whom you talk to, even the experts, regarding the type of compost they use, each one has a different reply. Nevertheless all would probably mention an open loam or seed compost with added grit, a touch of dolomite lime or carbonate of lime; and as long as grit and lime are added to any of your own chosen compost, your chances of a successful result will be higher.

First time pinks – an exciting time.

SEED SOWING

When sowing the seed, give only a light covering of compost or vermiculite, as sowing too deep will prevent germination. Water with the lightest of sprays so as not to bury the seed too deep or wash them up; cheshunt compound can be added to the water to help ward off the dreaded damping-off disease. Cover the pot with glass, or use clingfilm, then place in a light position out of the sun at a temperature of 16°C (62°F).

As soon as the seedlings are showing their first true leaves, prick them out into small pots: this individual attention gives them a wonderful start. When they reach approximately 12–15cm (5–6in) high, take out the growing tip to encourage bushiness. As soon as the roots show signs of filling the container, pot on into a good compost as mentioned above, feed with liquid fertilizer or any type of feed you are happy with, and stake the stems with thin canes if the need arises.

SEEDLING SELECTION

Now the seedlings begin to unfold their hidden beauty, and all the time and effort expended on all the preparations is rewarded during the next week or two as the first buds open to show their colour, whether they are fully double, single, or in between, in short their true finery. This is the time of assessment and of selection, not only of the best blooms, but also for any attributes in any of the seedlings that are considered valuable for future use in the breeding programme.

When pollen from single plants is used on a double plant to produce seed, it can only be expected that many of the seedlings will be single-flowered. However, most of these singles have the genes from the double parent, and when used again with a double plant will give a higher percentage of double flowers. So take a good look at the singles or semi-doubles with quality, that can be taken forward to the next breeding stage. Many seedlings are reluctant to, or incapable of passing on any pollen, and this is normal; but occasionally a single or semi-double will give generously, and a cluster of stamens high in the centre of the flower will be just laden with the magical grains.

If a flower splits its calyx, and all the flowers on that plant have the same defect, destroy it: this is a bad fault and must be eliminated. There is one exception to this, namely if the bloom has so many petals that the calyx has split under their pressure; in this instance watch the secondary flowers on the stem, because if these do not split their calyx, then the plant is a 'bull-nosed' bloom. These plants are very useful, because when used as the seed parent and crossed with single or semi-double flowers, good doubles can be produced with fewer petals than the parent, and showing first class quality with no sign of the split calyx.

BACK CROSSING

The difficult task now is to select the best of the seedlings and back-cross to the best parent, or to another of the best seedlings. This cross usually highlights any attributes or indeed any shortcomings, and good plants from these crosses will be the foundation for future breeding. If a particular colour or a type appears, this can be self-crossed by using pollen from another flower on the same plant: this will use the same bank of genes, and is more likely to produce the same colour again. There is no guarantee on this, but previous experience favours this approach and when

ABOVE: *Good open-bloomed seedlings.*

LEFT AND BELOW: *New seedlings on trial.*

another similar colour shows from this cross, use this to back-cross again, so multiplying the chances of this favourite colour dominating this line.

The alternative is to crossbreed haphazardly, as does one successful breeder, who splashes any pollen onto any available stigma to produce hundreds, maybe thousands of seedlings, and plants them on three allotments. He has winners, but they are few and far between, with a multitude of nondescripts all destined for the bonfire. Even so, the winners he gets cannot be used as foundation stock because he has no idea from which plant they came.

Use the line-breeding method, keep good records, and success is assured.

Primulas

Measure of difficulty	Crossing stage	Flower to seed	Seed germination	Seedling stage
FAIRLY EASY	EASY	EASY	EXPERIENCE	FAIRLY EASY

SITES FOR BEST RESULTS Certain types grow best in the greenhouse or conservatory, but hardy types such as primroses, polyantha and the like grow almost anywhere, in the shade, open ground, in grass or borders. During the plants' season of flowering the leaves are off the trees and the grass is shorter because of the time of year.

SPECIAL NOTES The F2 generation gives a far better mixture than the F1 generation, with more colours.

The primulas that generally come to mind are the polyanthus and primroses grown outdoors, with obconica and sinensis belonging to a greenhouse or indoors. These are the usual varieties grown by the general public, who do not realize that many hundreds of different species are available from dozens of nurseries throughout the country.

You only have to go back twenty years to the dominance of the polyanthus. They were without doubt the mainstay of the spring bulbs in parks, as well as in the majority of garden displays, because of their hardiness and the enormous colour variation they possess. At that time the colour range of the primrose was rather more limited, but this was about to change: brilliant manipulation on the genetic structure of the species, and in particular the colour variation, by the plant breeder has transformed it out of all expectations. This primrose is

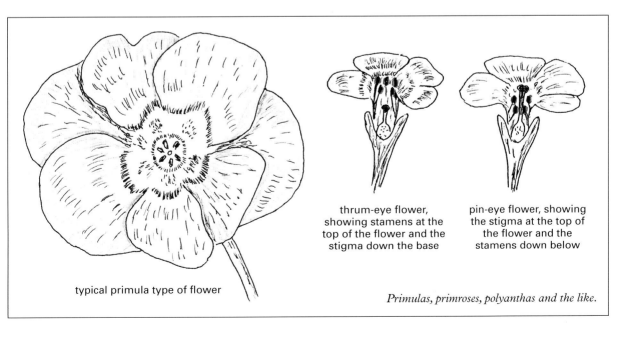

typical primula type of flower

thrum-eye flower, showing stamens at the top of the flower and the stigma down the base

pin-eye flower, showing the stigma at the top of the flower and the stamens down below

Primulas, primroses, polyanthas and the like.

now a top seller on Mother's Day, and dominates the spring bedding programme, and this is mainly due to the hybridist's perseverance.

There is a widespread diversity of every characteristic feature in the vast family of the primula species, something to please every hybridist whatever the line of crossbreeding he is following, from arid-loving plants to bog dwellers and every situation in between. Opportunity abounds in this species to create something special with an abundance of differing forms – habits for all conditions and a kaleidoscope of colours – in fact a dream plant for the plant breeder.

HISTORICAL DETAILS

The main historical details to interest the hybridist will undoubtedly be those that affected its development from the vast number of species to the modern-day overwhelming array of varieties. There is no lack of choice with the wonderful primula, and the delicate, tender look of the plant belies the hardiness inbred for centuries. The resilience of the primrose is amazing, that she can be frozen solid in the early morning, then showing off her full beauty soon after sunrise, evidently quite unaffected by her ordeal.

Some of the earliest recordings of note were from a Mr John Parkinson in the early 1600s, who described a plant in his writings that was thought to be the polyanthus, or in his own words 'a primrose-flowered cowslip'. Later that century there was a mention of a red primrose found in Turkey, which could have been the forefather of our modern-day coloured primroses.

As far back as the early 1500s, plant collectors went out all over the globe in search of more wonderful species of every type of plant available. It was a time when the landowners and the wealthy would employ men to travel the world, returning with a cargo of new introductions of seeds, plants and roots. Amongst them were indeed an almost endless supply of variation, and with each delivery other primulas surfaced: *Primula denticulata* was introduced by Dr J. Forbes Royal, *Primula mollis* by J.T. Booth, *Primula obconica* by C. Maries, to mention only a few. Great plant production of the new

species introduced was soon to stir more interest in the rich, anxious to be the ones to own perhaps the only plant in the country, or be the first to possess such a prize.

It was only a short period of time before the hybridizing of all the varied species came under the influence of the plant breeder creating the wealth of variety of the lovely primula family.

The genus family of the primula is one of the largest on record, being divided not only into species, but into sections of flower formation, leaf types, and also the differences required in habitat conditions. All these varying species are listed in the Pax System, which classifies the primula into thirty sections. Each of these sections again contains hundreds of varieties, so it can be appreciated that when selecting the parents of your dream cross, you are really spoilt for choice. More varieties are to be created, of this there is no doubt, with such a wealth of breeding material on hand waiting for manipulation.

If you are indulging for the first time, it would be advisable to cross like with like to gain easy success, trying the more elaborate crossings at a later date – although many new creations have resulted from the hit-or-miss method. However, it is wise to gain experience from the commoner types in order to build confidence in one's own ability – there is nothing more disheartening than to fail at the very first attempt. You will feel greatly encouraged after the first success, and have a sense of great achievement.

PARENT SELECTION

A more relaxed approach can be made to the primula in the selection of the parents, many other plants requiring very particular statistics to comply with show bench standards. And, although we need to be aware of keeping the standard of the primula to the highest degree possible, this species has a quality that filters through to the smallest detail, producing first class material almost constantly. Careful examination of the plants will show any minor defects that will be detrimental to the structure of the next generation, and obviously stock of poor constitution must be discarded.

HYBRIDIZING

The key to primula crossbreeding is understanding the structure of the flower. Study the formation of a number of blooms, and you will see that the stigma and stamens of the reproductive organs are of two types known as the pin-eyed type and the thrum-eyed type. In the pin-eyed, or pinhead type, the flowers bear a tall stigma to the top of the flower, but the stamens are way down to the base of the floret. In the thrum-eyed or thrum-head type, the stigma is way down in the floret and the stamens are at the top. A knowledge of the differing types is helpful to the breeding programme, and by taking a close look into the floret of any primula, primrose, polyanthus,

or even the auricula, you will recognize if it is a pin-eye, where the centre of the flower is either a pin head with a tiny single knob, or a thrum-eye, where there is a ring of stamens just inside the lip of the floret. If a single floret is taken from the flower and one petal torn down, you will see from the inner parts the type of structure it possess.

Also notice that the stamens are attached to the petals. If crossbreeding is to take place, these stamens must be removed before the pollen is released from them; this emasculation leaves the stigma fully intact and ready to be pollinated with pollen from the other selected parent. Either type of plant can be used in whichever combination is preferred, but if this operation takes place in an insect-free

Pin-eye flower to the left, thrum-eye flower to the right.

Petals are removed to show the different types of flower.

room indoors, or perhaps the greenhouse, then the procedure can be completed without tearing down the petals, as long as the pin-eye is used as the seed parent. It will be obvious that using the pin-eye with the stigma at the top of the floret will give easy access to make the cross.

It has been my experience that better plants are obtained from thrum to pin combination, although by tearing down the petals, the stigmas in either type will be exposed ready to receive pollen. Sometimes the stigmas are ripe immediately, but more often than not, a day or two later gives more favourable results.

Fertilization occurs soon after pollination, and Mother Nature continues the work by developing the seed: the swelling of the ovary indicates that all is proceeding as it should. Ripening time is around July, depending on the time of the cross and naturally the prevailing weather and growing conditions, so watch for the browning of the seedpod. Mark all your crosses, because the pods are usually covered by other flowers on the plant, and some species tend

to turn the pod downwards, so it looks as if there are no pods there at all. Some also have very small pods in the centre of big leafy sepals that almost hide them from view; perhaps these irregularities are nature's way of protecting the seeds from birds.

As the seedpod ripens, take it off, together with a small section of stem, and place it in a paper bag; the pod is like a small transparent ball, and sometimes the seed is visible through the film case. Using this method the seed will soon ripen fully.

THE SEED

Now you must decide whether to sow the seed immediately or save it until the spring. One important factor relative to the primula is the fact that high temperatures are detrimental to its germination, in particular if you decide to store it over the winter. Any seed subject to a temperature of 20°C (70°F) or more, whether sown or stored, can become dormant and so delay or even prevent germination. When only a few seedlings appear from a batch of good quality seed, this is usually the reason. The seed is very small and only requires to be sown on the soil surface; then cover it with limestone grit – this is to hold the seed in place, and also to deter the growth of algae and lichen.

When fresh seed is sown, a good germination can be expected, unless it is a variety that requires stratification – this means it will only germinate after a cold period such as a winter, or a month to six weeks in the fridge. The majority of primula seedlings, even after germination, develop slowly, and patience is required while you wait for them to reach the pricking out stage. In fact it would be wise to leave the seedlings to stand in their pots and to overwinter in a favourable position, rather than prick them out singly with no time to develop a better root system, particularly if winter is approaching.

If a cold greenhouse or a cold frame is available, the seed pots can be placed in these to overwinter; this method usually gives them a good start by January or February, and at the very latest, March. It is helpful to water them often with clean rainwater: this happens in the wild, and helps to break the dormancy. Use a very fine spray so as not to disturb the position of the seed.

Seed pods ripening.

Seedlings pricked out.

THE SEEDLINGS

Once the seedlings are potted on and growing well, they will require a hardening off period before they are planted out in the garden. A liquid feed with a formula that is high in nitrogen will give the greenery a boost; although they are not gross feeders, the feed at half strength will give the young plants a flying start. Once the plant has grown to the required size, then a half feed of low nitrogen, high potash will help to harden it off, leaving it in prime condition to bloom to its heart's content.

It has been stated at times that primulas do not respond to feeding; this is not true, however, and is a fallacy that perhaps stems from the fact that many primula species live on bare rock in the mountains with no soil to succour them; but these surely find the feed elements they require from the rain washing from the rocks. Also bear in mind that these plants possess very few leaves but an abundance of flowers. If a high nitrogen feed is given just as a boost, then changed to potash, you will have a large healthy specimen that will produce a luxurious crop of flowers.

F1 SELECTION

If the crosses made were from two different species, then the F1 seedlings will be very varied, in leaf, type and colour – each will be an individual. However, it is from this assorted collection that an assessment of quality will have to be made. Most of the plants will betray some sort of small fault, and some more than others, but we need select only the very best plants with which to make a further cross. Self-crossing the best of the seedlings will supply the F2 generation, which is where the quality will show if any exits; also crossing the best seedling back to the best of the parents or between two sister seedlings – these are the crosses that are most likely to supply something special.

When your ideal seedling arrives it is easy enough to propagate by taking cuttings, or even better by splitting; these are the only ways to multiply your selected seedling and to keep identical plants, especially at this early stage. Seed from the seedling will result in the F3 generation, when another batch of varying types will appear, except this time the new plants will have a closer resemblance to the chosen F1 seedling. By selecting from each batch of seedlings the plant most like your F1 selection, and self-crossing each generation, it will be possible to fix the strain so that the seeds saved will all turn out like peas in a pod, or near enough. At this stage you can say your own strain is fixed. By using these methods and introducing colours of quality into the strain, you will create a wonderful garden display that is the envy of your friends and neighbours.

Roses

The sight of a garden without a rose is indeed very rare, and even neglected gardens, chest high in nettles and brambles, will most likely have a rose pushing through somewhere. A garden display will usually have not only bush and floribunda roses, but climbers, old shrub roses and ramblers. With such a variety of types, as well as the variation in growth habits – and not counting the wide spectrum of colour – it is no wonder the rose is undoubtedly the queen of the flower world. Fossil remains tell us that many plants were in existence many thousands of years ago, and over the centuries the rose has contributed to the making of perfumes, medicinal aids and vitamin additions; and we know from drawings it was also used to counteract the smells in the caves of the cave dwellers.

The rose, like many other species of plant, was found only in the northern hemisphere, and was transported and introduced to the southern hemisphere, at a time when Man was fully aware of its qualities and the great desire to plant it on the other side of the world. Roses in those days would have been quite different from the roses we know today, not only through nature's elaborate development in the way she uses insects, and bees in particular, also because of the mutations that tend to appear out of nowhere and give a new direction in style or colour, thereby adding to the genetic variation of the species. Man has undoubtedly changed the plant world with his inquisitive manipulating in his search for something new – but this is human nature, and a hundred years from now the rose, amongst other things, will surely have changed again to reveal even greater surprises.

THE FIRST STEPS

The idea of adding to the already beautiful and magnificent range of roses available would appear to be a daunting task. Indeed it treads a path of uncertainty and disappointment – but to the true hybridist this is the challenge he expects and without it the thrill of success would be worthless. The beginner would be wise to read a book on the species to try to comprehend the enormous variety of material available to the hybridist. Creating a lovely rose is maybe a step towards the fulfilment of a dream, but the fact that the rose has been inbred, outbred and crossed in so many ways, like many other plants for a number of years, means it has a very complex genetic structure.

Professionals claim that at least a thousand seedlings are thrown away before a true show-stopper appears amongst the crop – daunting odds for an amateur breeder, and even more so for a beginner. Yet the list of successful amateur breeders of top class roses has grown longer every year, and amateurs surely don't have either the room or the time to grow so many seedlings. This is a very encouraging position for the newcomer, and self-belief will assist in creating the rose of your dreams.

A good many plants today have a healthy resistance to disease, handed down from the hardy wild varieties, and blended into modern roses by the skill of the early plant breeders. This is one of the essential attributes that must be maintained until it becomes a dominant feature in every generation of plants. In selecting the parent plants, use only the healthiest of stock: if both have inherited a resistance, then the future seedlings are likely to possess the same. And whether a cross between two plants or a self-cross is undertaken, you can expect seedlings of equal merit.

Due to the complexity of their genetic make-up, a surprise mixed bag can be expected with any combinations and many pleasant arrivals into the bargain. At this stage the thrill of seeing the flower for the first time is just the same if the seedling is a good or a poor specimen: the later assessment is the time for elation or disappointment – but remember that plant breeding in certain areas, and particularly this one, is a lottery, and whether good or bad, the new seedling is your creation and yours alone, with no other rose identical to it.

THE CROSS

The first step is to decide on the rose that will be the seed parent; then select a bud that shows just a hint of colour as the sepals part. Open the bud very gently to take away the petals; in many varieties this leaves the stamens and the stigmas in close proximity, in some others they are quite separate. The stamens are then removed with either tweezers or a small pair of scissors. Sometimes the immature stamens are packed so close to the immature stigmas that an extra few hours may be needed to allow them to separate before emasculation can take place; but these must be removed before pollen is shed, to keep the immature stigmas clean.

The stamens grow in a circle around the centre mound that holds the stigmas, and can be taken or cut away completely; it is important that no trace of pollen is left on the stigmas, and a magnifying glass will be most helpful to ensure the success of this operation. Cover the bud to protect it from

The ideal bud to be emasculated.

The petals are removed leaving the stigma and young stamens.

foreign pollen until your selected pollen can be applied to the ripe stigmas: these will show a glistening on the tips when they are ripe, when they can be given a thorough dusting with the selected

Stamens removed leaving stigma ready to be pollinated.

Complete head of pollen bud, put on a saucer to ripen for later use.

Stamens removed. If placed in a saucer all pollen will be released the next day.

Do not forget to keep name tags with pollen as well as pollinated buds.

pollen; then cover again for a few days. When taking off the immature stamens, place them on a saucer with a label, and in a few hours they will mature and the pollen will be ripe, and ready to apply to another flower. If this practice is followed on both of the flowers selected, the pollen and the stigmas will be ripe on both flowers, and the cross can be completed on both at the same time. Most important is to label the crosses as they are made, with parents and dates, and as usual the seed parent first, then the pollen parent.

Another successful way to apply pollen is to place a cardboard toilet roll centre over the emasculated bud to half way down its length, then press the cardboard tube in until it lies against the stem, and hold it there with a clothes peg. Into the open top half, place a bud of the selected pollen flower with the petals removed but the stamens still on, even if these are still immature. The top bud can be held by the stem by another clothes peg, thus closing the top of the toilet roll tube. Leave for a few days, giving a slight tap each day; this will ensure that a good pollination takes place. If it is possible, the top bud can be replaced to ensure more ripe pollen is available. Most stems can hold this apparatus quite well, but if a plant is weak, a cane can be used; this not only keeps the pollen dry, but keeps intruders away.

HARVESTING

All has gone well, pegs and tube have been removed from the pregnant bud, and now we wait for the ripening of the hips. In an unpredictable summer the hip will never in fact ripen; but if this operation

Seed pod almost ready to harvest.

Rose seed.

is undertaken at the commencement of the flowering season, then better results can be expected. A favourable practice is for the intended parents to be potted up early in the season; they can be secured under glass where they can continue to grow if the weather takes a turn for the worse. As soon as the hips – or 'heps' as some people like to call them – are ripe, take them to the sink and open them in water to release the seeds: these will be mostly cream- or chocolate-coloured and more than likely misshapen, and they need to be washed in running water to wash away the pulp, which if it gets on your skin is very irritating. Once cleaned, the seeds are soaked in a fungicide liquid or a weak solution of bleach, then placed in a plastic bag with a good handful of dampened vermiculite.

Place the details on a label in with the seed, and then seal the bag; then place it somewhere warm – a greenhouse or airing cupboard will do – and leave for six weeks. After this period of time, place it in the bottom of the fridge in the salad compartment for two months. By this time we are nearing late winter, say February, which is the ideal time to bring them in from the cold: separate them from the vermiculite and sow in potting compost in the usual way; then place them in the greenhouse or on a windowsill, and germination can be expected in a few weeks.

It is an exciting time when the green cotyledons first peep through the compost, to be followed by the shoot and the first leaves – and this is a very crucial time for the seedling. Many are lost during this period because of damping-off disease, so clean, sterilized compost is essential. To ensure a perfect start for the seedling, use only cooled boiled water with an addition of fungicide in a weaker solution, then dampen the surface with a fine spray. Healthy specimens can then be confidently expected rather than just hoped for. From the time of germination to when the first flowers show colour will be about eight weeks, and by then the seedling will be between 10–15cm (4–6in) high.

Do not expect all the seedlings to grow up together – they have a mind of their own and will appear when they are ready, some much later than others. So when the first ones are pricked out of the pot, be careful not to disturb any other seed that may not have started, but leave them undisturbed to make an entrance later.

Rose seedlings.

Two rose seedlings waiting for the first flower.

THE END PRODUCT

The colour shown in the seedling flower is usually the colour of the mature flower, though the pastel shades tend to deepen as the plant matures. The petal situation can be more precarious, but generally more petals appear as each flower opens – though sometimes they don't. The scent can develop as the plant matures, so if a slight whiff is suspected in the early stages, then there is hope for a full fragrance as time goes by. If the plant is of good merit, bud it onto rose stock and bed it out to trial it in garden conditions: this environment will prove its qualities or highlight its shortcomings. A first class plant can be multiplied either by taking cuttings or by grafting onto rose stock. You know by now the procedure by which to progress to the next generation, and if your experience has developed, and you cross the best with the best, then the world is your oyster.

Sweet Peas

SIMPLICITY GUIDE

Measure of difficulty	Crossing stage	Flower to seed	Seed germination	Seedling stage
CAN BE TRICKY	EXPERIENCE	EASY	EASY	EASY

SITES FOR BEST RESULTS For exhibition blooms, choose an open site and train in the cordon style, in rich, well manured ground just on the alkaline side of neutral. For growing in the bush method, almost anywhere in an open site.
SPECIAL NOTES Starting the growing cycle in October allows the seedlings to develop a good root system before planting out in March. Early flowers with good long stems is the result, with the bonus of having an earlier crop of seed.

Most ladies fall in love with the elegant sweet pea. It has such fascinating flowers, with the most delicate of perfume, plus the final accolade that the more blooms that are picked, the more are produced: a gem of a plant. The species always tends to give the impression of tenderness, frailty, and delicacy with elegance, but it is in fact a very tough and resilient plant, capable of withstanding even the frost for a short period. The fact that the seedlings are grown in a cold frame with only matting as protection against the most severe weather, authenticates its hardiness.

HISTORY

It seems unbelievable that the sweet pea was unheard of in England until midway through the seventeenth century. Although it is thought to have originated in Malta, the first seed came from Sicily, sent by a Sicilian priest Francis Cupani to Dr Uvedale, of Enfield, Middlesex. These early plants would most likely have been of the type we find in some gardens growing wild and self-seeding each year, showing the hardiness of their predecessors but of the common mauve colour, and definitely lacking the quality and colours of the modern varieties.

Very little is recorded as to the development of the species until the beginning of the nineteenth century, when several colours appeared: this boosted its popularity, although it was by then quite widely grown for its fragrance, and because of its encouraging response to good husbandry. Towards the end of the nineteenth century a man by the name of Eckland transformed the flower into a popular plant, helping, amongst others, to create new varieties or novelties. One variety was at the time named a 'Grandiflora' type because of the larger petals, especially the standards or back petals. One of his introductions, namely his 'Prima Donna', was the best plant of its day, and it was from 'Prima Donna' that several mutations evolved, all apparently around the same period. On each occasion the mutation produced a wavy-petalled flower, prettier and larger than anything before. This gave rise to two different types or strains: one was the Unwin type, the other the Spencer type, the latter becoming more popular owing to its larger size and wavier petals.

By the year 1900, the sweet pea was becoming so popular that keen growers decided to found 'the National Sweet Pea Society', and it was soon evident from the enrolment figures that there was great interest in the flower. The society and its members have played a major role in its development and distribution, as well as in teaching the skills of expert showmanship. They have contributed immensely to the quality and popularity of the plant, and have given generously of their experience; indeed we are indebted to all the previous members for contributing to the pleasures we enjoy today. Nevertheless, this is safe in the knowledge that the present members will reliably supply the same good will for future sweet pea enthusiasts.

HYBRIDIZING

One thing in favour of hybridizing the sweet pea is the fact that seeds can be sown in the same season that they are produced: a blessing for the impatient breeder. Furthermore, it is a simple enough flower to cross-pollinate once the mechanics of the bloom are mastered. The intricacies of the petals are the key to success in the self-pollinating of the flower, whether left to its own devices or assisted by passing insects; moreover this method will always produce the same clone flower once the plant has been fixed. This cycle will go on year after year until something or someone changes the course of nature – and our plan is to do just that.

The first important factor on the trail to the new sweet pea is to start with the best quality parent plant possible. Select good, strong, healthy specimens, as these assets will be passed on to the new seedlings, along with the quality genes as well as the undesirable characteristics that most plants possess. The best way to examine the types of flower that you intend to use as parents is to visit shows that exhibit top class varieties. A close look at the prize winners will reveal the varying technicalities of each plant, and these are the characteristics that must be blended together to create a seedling with all the finer points that will lead to perfection.

Many winners on the showbench are special plants that have perhaps not been released on the market, but if you talk to the exhibitor you may be lucky enough to be able to buy some seed from him, or find out where to buy the seed. Most exhibitors will consider it an honour that someone thought so much of their plants to ask about them, and will be pleased to talk about them.

Once a decision has been made as to the parent plants, the next step is to acquire the seed from a reputable sweet pea specialist or an exhibitionist friend. Grow the plants in a favourable sunny position, with a view to ripening the seed expected from the crosses you value most.

MAKING THE CROSS

As the cross-pollinating techniques were explained earlier, the next step is taken when the flowers are quite abundant on the vines. Allow two or three stems to open fully before attempting to perform the cross-pollinating; this is because the first couple of stems often drop buds, but the third is more stable. This would also be a good time to practise pulling down the keel of the flower to expose the stigma and stamens. By examining several flowers at different stages, the ideal bud condition will be self-evident. If the stamens are still too immature to release pollen, then you should emasculate the flower (remove the stamens).

To do this, take a large unopened bloom by gently holding the keel in the right thumb and forefinger, nipping only the very bottom; this is important because the sexual parts are in this area. With the left thumb and finger, pull back the upper petals; this leaves the keel exposed enough to tear down the side, making the removal of the stamens an easy operation. If the stamens in fact shed their pollen during this exercise, then use the next flower up the stem.

Many ways have been tried to transport the pollen to the stigma, and this is one of them: use a flower that has recently opened, and pull down the keel with the left hand, at the same time holding the

The ideal bud to emasculate.

ABOVE: *Flower opened to show the stigma and stamens.*

ABOVE RIGHT: *Stamens removed and the stigma is ready to receive pollen.*

RIGHT: *Pollen flower.*

thumb and finger of the right hand at the tip of the keel. This jets the ripe pollen onto your thumb and finger, which will then carry the pollen to the ripe stigma. The stigma can easily be coated on both sides by gentle stroking, making sure that the tip has most of it, so completing the pollination. If time permits, a repeat performance the next day will most certainly ensure success.

It is advisable to label all crosses made, putting the female (seed parent) first and the male (pollen parent) second; this is the usual procedure in plant breeding. If only one or two florets are crossed on the same stem, take off the remainder so that all the seed on that particular stem is from your cross. Using the pedigree helps you to plan future crossings in the breeding programme ahead. Early crossing is advised, to allow time in the season for the seed to ripen; anyone contemplating this activity would be advised to use autumn-sown seeds. As the seed ripens, keep the crosses separate by giving them either a code number or a name; also keep all succeeding generations, recording them in detail in a stud book.

It is of great advantage to allow the seedpods to ripen fully on the vine: the seed reaches full size, and will possess the full vigour required for optimum performance. Seed from under-ripe pods will fail in one way or another, and is not worth the trouble.

SEED SOWING

Once the seed is fully ripe and dried, save it in cool, dry conditions until required. It is advisable to start the seeds off in October of the same year as the ripening, as this gives time for the seedlings to build a good strong root system before the onset of winter. This method should give 100 per cent success. Don't grow too many of each variety – twenty of each is probably ideal; if you have an abundance of seed from any special plant it is not feasible to grow them all, because growing too many will make scrutinizing each individual plant a tedious occupation rather than a hobby.

ABOVE: *Successful pods developing.*

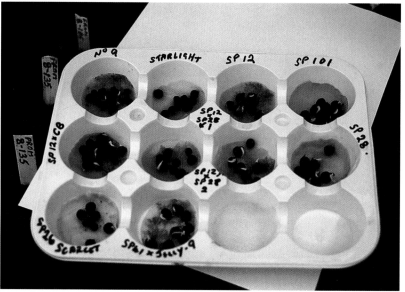

Seeds started in trays show 100 per cent germination.

GERMINATING AND GROWING ON

Cut three circles of kitchen paper and place them on a saucer, pour on some boiling water, then drain off the excess. Place the seeds – these will have been soaked in mild bleach water for a couple of hours to sterilize them – onto the wet paper, and cover with one more layer of kitchen paper. If they are put in a warm place and the paper kept moist at all times but not under water, they will germinate in four days: the radical root will show first, then two days later the first green shoot will appear. At this stage they can be sown individually into plastic cups: cut holes in the bottom of these, then fill them with good potting compost. When sowing the germinated seed, make a hole 2.5cm (1in) deep with a dibber, and drop the seed, with the root facing downwards into the hole, and gently cover it over. The seed will send up the true stem in two or three days' time if placed in the same warm place.

Close up of tray germination.

BELOW: *Seedlings planted out.*

Immediately the shoots show through the soil, harden off the seedlings a little day by day until they are hardy enough to place in the cold frame or cool greenhouse; make sure they are placed in the lightest position to grow, to secure strong, healthy, stocky seedlings. If the plants grow more the 15cm (6in) in the frame or greenhouse, take out the growing tip to encourage side shoots. If grown in these conditions until March or April, they can be planted in their flowering position – you will be surprised to see the lovely root system gained by this method. Plant them in front of their canes, and if possible, tie loosely. Let them develop for a couple of weeks, then get down on your hands and knees to examine the stem near the ground. Take a good look at the side shoots from the stem, and you will see that some are thin and dry at the base: these were the first ones to form, and are brittle and will never be good stems to use. Select a side shoot that looks plump and juicy, because this will carry all the nutrients required for a healthy plant; the older, dried up one will be the longest side shoot, but the shorter plump one will overtake it very quickly. Take off all the other side shoots, leaving just the selected one, and tie it in to the cane. Autumn sowing will bring early flowers and early ripe seeds in plenty.

F1 HYBRIDS: FIRST GENERATION

The following season gives the results of the original crosses, and these plants are the F1 hybrids, the children of the first cross. Don't expect too much change at this stage, as many will show very similar characteristics to the parents; the seedlings may be similar in colour, although they may be different from the parents. If you sow the seed from this F1 cross it will produce the F2 generation; this will give a varied colour range if parents of a different colour were used, but if parents of similar colours were used, then more of that colour would be forthcoming in the offspring.

Similarity is normal in the first generation, but we look forward to allowing the seedlings to flower and produce the self-pollinated seed ready for the following year, from which we can expect the changes in both colour and characteristics, perhaps some better, but also some less so. This is the time to scrutinize the new seedlings, discarding any that show unfavourable traits, whether affecting growth or colour, or with any adverse peculiarities. On the plus side, promising seedlings may be expected, and can be retained. The quality plants can be allowed to produce the F3 hybrid, and if it proves to be fixed, it will produce the same clone plant every year that it is allowed to self-pollinate: this will be your new sweet pea.

Experience in cross-breeding is feeling when to do certain things at certain times, and conveying this sense of timing into words is not so conclusive as the practical operation. Of greatest value is the experience gained by practising the emasculation of the flower, on buds at different stages of development. The important part of this procedure can be mastered in such a short time, and is invaluable to the success of cross-breeding.

FIXING THE SEEDLING

When you are happy that the right seedling has arrived, allow its flower to set seed – in other words allow it to self-pollinate; keep the seeds separate, and sow them in autumn in the usual way. This time when the flowers arrive they should all look alike, and if not, then you must repeat the whole procedure of selecting seed from the ones that do look alike, and growing them on to the next generation. Most new seedlings fix after a couple of seasons, and some do so almost at once, but then again some are really frustrating and take many seasons. I had one that was a lovely multicoloured flower, but which gave a different variation every season until I gave it up as a lost cause; luckily for us, however, most of them fix eventually.

Grow as many of the seedlings as possible so as to eliminate any rogues still lurking in the genetic background; it is far better to purify the variety before it goes to trial, because a rogue will nullify your chance of success. It is wise to test your own seedling against others, perhaps at the local flower shows, or to grow it on alongside an established named variety, to compare the quality of your flower.

FRUIT AND VEGETABLES

Potatoes

SIMPLICITY GUIDE

Measure of difficulty	Crossing stage	Flower to seed	Seed germination	Seedling stage
EXPERIENCE	FAIRLY DIFFICULT	EASY	EASY	EASY

SITES FOR BEST RESULTS A well manured area with good drainage is all that is required. New seeds can be grown in pots to supply the baby tubers for first year planting.

SPECIAL NOTES Cross the flowers in the same way as with tomatoes, to produce the small apple-like fruits. Master the crossing stage, and the rest is easy.

Many readers will be surprised to hear that I consider it an easy matter to produce a new variety of potato. Not that every potato plant will meet the standards necessary to conform to modern-day quality, far from it; so we have to scrutinize every stage of development in order to reach a final product that is worthy of being called an excellent potato variety.

This vegetable has been one of the mainstay food products of many civilizations in the [South] American continent for thousands of years, even before the golden years of the Inca civilization during which the potato was well established. There is evidence of these vegetables being a staple food crop in writings way back in time, and it is unbelievable that it took until half way through the sixteenth century before the potato was brought to Europe. It first arrived in Spain during the Spanish Conquest, and because it was so easy to cultivate, it was soon to spread throughout the rest of the European countries. There has always been the belief that Sir Walter Raleigh brought the potato to England.

No doubt the potato of that period would have been of a different nature from the varieties we use today. I often wonder what took its place before its introduction, as you can imagine the dilemma that would surround our everyday meals today if the potato vanished for a few years.

There was famine in Ireland in 1845 when the potato harvest was devastated by a fungus, which resulted in thousands of people starving to death. And in the seventeenth century, potato blight is known to have wiped out acres of crops, not only in Ireland but all over Europe. Fortunately some measure of resistance has been bred into the modern varieties, and fungicide sprays are used as protection against disease. This is a lesson to remember, that the top priority is to use only healthy, disease-free plants when selecting the foundation stock for a future breeding programme.

STOCK SELECTION

There is more to selecting the parental varieties than one might at first anticipate. There is colour preference, shape, whether you want an early, mid-season or late variety, and texture is also vital to the cooking methods intended, whether you want a floury or a waxy type. The waxy potato is good for boiling as they hold their shape and do not crumble, and the floury varieties are ideal for chips and for baked potatoes – but every one has his own favourite, so what you want as an end product will have some bearing on the variety you select. Test the cooking qualities first, to find your favourite texture, because this quality will most likely be passed down to the new seedlings – although there is no guarantee of this. With the texture quality you prefer already in one parent, it is your personal taste that is the next step in the process.

Typical potato flowers.

BELOW: *Ideal bud to be emasculated.*

BOTTOM: *Some petals removed to reveal stamens lying alongside stigma.*

PLANTING

Plant the selected tubers in containers so that cross-breeding can take place anywhere that the containers can be moved to – on a bench, in the greenhouse or on a table, as having the flowers at close proximity will make your work easier. Place the containers in the greenhouse if an early start is to be made, though don't forget to harden the plants off before standing them outside. Grow outdoors until the flowers show on the haulm, when they can be brought into the greenhouse for convenience. Like all plants, potatoes grow better in outdoor conditions. As the potato is a relation of the tomato, it will come as no surprise that the flower not only looks like the tomato flower, but is treated in the same way as far as crossbreeding is concerned.

THE CROSS

Select a flower still in the bud stage, with the petals closed. It is possible to take the tweezers and gently grip the petals close to the base of the flower

Stamens removed leaving stigma to ripen.

Stigma ready to accept pollen from male flower.

Flowers to supply male pollen.

bud, holding the stem with the other hand. Gently pull the petals up, away from the stem; this snaps them all off in one pull, so they slide gently off the stigma, leaving this intact. If done at the right time, it will also take away the stamens that are connected to the petals, before their pollen is placed on the stigma. Take note that the stigma stands up in the centre of the bud, so try to grip the petals at the side so as not to damage it. Most important now is to examine the tip of the stigma with a magnifying lens, looking for any sign of pollen on the sticky surface. If the tip is clean, we can go on to the final stage, but if there is any doubt whatsoever, and you think that some pollen may have touched the vital point, then forget that bud and try the next one up the truss. You have to be certain that the cross is pure, otherwise imagine the time you will waste. If the stigma is in a clean condition, then the pollen from the other selected plant can be applied – as long as the stigma is in a ripe condition, which may be the same day or a day or two later. Examination of the stigma tip will reveal a sticky surface, which indicates the time is right.

Applying the pollen to the stigma can be achieved in several ways. One way is to take a flower that has just opened, gently pluck off the petals plus stamens as before, and then very carefully slip them onto the lone stigma of the other flower. If this is done carefully, the loose flower head can be left in position until petals wither, by which time the pollen should have pollinated the seed flower; examination of the stigma, and particularly the small fruit at its base, will confirm a fertilization, or a failure. If several buds have been pollinated at the offset, then one of them should show the results you want. Placing the flower petals plucked from the pollen parent to the lone stigma of the proposed seed parent is a very delicate operation, needing care and steady hands, but it is undoubtedly the best and the most successful method – a second plucked flower can take the place of the first one if this withers too quickly.

An alternative method of placing pollen on the stigma, which may be better for the somewhat heavy-handed, is to place a finger tip at the end of the point of the flower, at the same time tapping the bloom gently with a finger from the other hand: if the pollen is in a ripe condition, it will drop onto the finger tip. Several flowers can be tapped until enough pollen is gathered. Take the finger to the stigma, and if the pollen is very carefully touched to the stigma tip, enough will adhere to achieve pollination. Label the cross before you forget which plant was pollinated by tying coloured cotton to the flower and marking a label in the pot to describe the cross.

SEED DEVELOPMENT

Although the potato fruit develops in the same way as the tomato, the fruit is more like a small green apple. This is left on the plant until it is in a ripe condition, and is then harvested, and the small seeds removed ready for sowing the following season in good seed compost. The seedlings develop very quickly once established, and are best sown individually in small pots in the greenhouse or windowsill. Harden off the seedlings with the intention of planting them out in prepared ground when all risk of frost has passed. Test the seedlings in the same way as ordinary tubers during the growing season.

FIRST POTATOES

It is better to put a code number to all the seedlings individually, because each one will have its own identity and will be different in some way to any other. The crucial time comes when harvesting, when it is essential to keep the product from each plant separate – you could place each crop from each plant in a separate bag – until you come to examine them. Note the weight and amount from each plant, because there is often a considerable difference between them. A plant producing a good heavy crop usually continues to do so in later plantings. Store in a cool, dark place.

TASTING TIME

Tasting the new potatoes, and assessing their qualities, is down to the preferences of the grower – we all have our favourite flavours. It must be realized that to give each variety an honest assessment, they have to be cooked separately, not all in the same pan, and must then be tasted one by one to assess properly the quality and the preferred flavour. Once a favourite is selected, all the tubers of that variety can be saved and a row planted the following season, giving a full crop from which to select the best for another season, whilst enjoying the flavours of your very own variety.

SELECTION

It is always wise not only to pick the best flavoured plant, but also to take special note of how it grows: for instance you might ask yourself, is it healthy? Is it prone to blight? Does it produce plenty of healthy crops? Are the potatoes the right shape and colour? All these things can be manipulated if each new variety is studied and assessed, and again crossed appropriately; it is a long way to perfection, but tasting the new crops is a most enjoyable pastime! We might also require a variation in the texture, whether waxy or fluffy, or a floury type of constitution, and these attributes can be blended as long as the selected parents possess the desired qualities.

As the crops of the seedlings are tasted, note the details of the eating qualities, and anything else of special value that may contribute to making a particular seedling worthy of becoming your permanent crop. It is important to start the programme with the types of potato preferred, and then manipulate these until perfection or satisfaction is in the cooking pot. And even if the temptation is to go for the oval, shallow-eyed, smooth-skinned variety, one main characteristic to concentrate on and blend with all the other attributes is disease resistance. Always look out for signs of virus, and if any are found, then it is not worth keeping these potatoes for the following season's crop. So when selecting your seed potatoes for next year's crop, plant only virus-free stock. One reason why Scottish-grown seed potatoes are best is because aphids, which are the main distributors of virus, are less plentiful because of the strong winds. A start with top-quality stock is one of the best ways to achieve excellence to be proud of.

Tomatoes

Measure of difficulty	Crossing stage	Flower to seed	Seed germination	Seedling stage
EXPERIENCE	FAIRLY DIFFICULT	EASY	EASY	EASY

SITES FOR BEST RESULTS Although most tomato plants are greenhouse grown, many hardier varieties grow well out in the open. Do not cross the hardier ones with the tender ones until more experienced. Good results can be expected.
SPECIAL NOTES Expect some varied flavours: some may have a horrid taste, as well as some lovely variations. No one else will have a tomato just like yours: it will be unique. Even in the second generation from seeds saved, more variations will arise.

This plant has changed dramatically since the days of its introduction into Europe. It grows wild as a weed in Peru where it still flourishes, spreading its creeping vines along the ground, covered in small but rather sharp-tasting fruits. Although there are many forms of tomato in Peru and other South American countries, almost all have the sharp flavour that has vanished from the modern varieties. This forerunner of the tomato we have today was first introduced into Europe in the mid-sixteenth century, and probably brought back by the Spanish and introduced into England by the end of that century. It was introduced over here more as a decorative plant, and was at first regarded as a poisonous species; later however, as its eating qualities were realized, it was known as the 'love apple' because of its claimed aphrodisiac capabilities.

The change in size and flavour, and the hardier qualities of the plant, can be placed firmly to the credit of the plant breeder. Greenhouses all over the country are bursting with the fruits of this weed from Peru, but many more newer varieties will certainly appear as the seasons go by.

PARENT SELECTION

Selecting the plants that will become the parents of your future masterpieces has to be one of the most considered choices you will ever make, in the hope of tracking down the right road to success. When studying the possible contenders, many aspects must be considered before the final pairings are made. First you must decide on the type, the colour, the shape and also the flavour: these are attributes in the genetic make-up of the parent that can be transferred to the offspring. The uncertainty of the combination of genes in the chromosomes inevitably makes the new seedling an exciting prospect, and selecting parent plants with favourable characteristics will give you a head start. Starting with two mediocre plants in the hope of achieving top quality offspring is a possibility, but many years, plus many heartaches will have to be endured before this comes about, not to mention the skill needed to accomplish it.

Mixing types, whether colours, or stripes, or round or plum shapes, gives an array of unstable variations that are very difficult to fix. Certainly this is the only path to tread if something completely original is required, but it will be a long one, and it will demand great patience, and the courage to withstand disappointments – but the sense of satisfaction when the prodigal seedling comes home will be great indeed.

The beginner would be advised to cross two closer types that have most of the required characteristics, at least until he or she has the benefit of a bit more courage and experience. By choosing two

The ideal bud is the bottom left one. The others are too open.

Applying the pollen to the stigma.

to the parents, but the majority will undoubtedly be inferior to both; this appears to be the norm, although there is also the possibility of a top quality variety emerging from the very first attempt.

HYBRIDIZING

Although it is possible to cross many plants growing in the open ground, the tomato is not to be considered for this treatment. Plants grown indoors, whether in the greenhouse or on the windowsill, are ideally placed to be cross-pollinated, where precise manipulations can be administered. Dealing with the tomato flower is a very delicate operation and requires a keen eye and intricate finger work; it is exactly the same method as for crossing the potato.

THE CROSS

Select the second or third truss of flowers to cross, examining the flower bud closely to use one that hasn't opened. Then take your tweezers and gently grip the yellow petals close to the base of the flower bud. Holding the stem with the other hand, gently pull the petals up; this will snap them off, and the whole head of yellow then slides up and off the stigma. This leaves the stigma intact, and if the bud has been selected at the right time, this operation will have taken away the stamens, too, before their pollen was placed on the stigma.

Now use a magnifying glass to examine the tip of the stigma, looking for any sign of yellow pollen on the sticky surface. If clean, then we can go on to the final stage, but if there is any doubt whatsoever that some pollen might have touched the vital point, then forget that bud and try the next one up the truss. You have to be certain that the cross is pure, otherwise the whole operation will have been a waste of time – you will be saving the seed to get the plant you already have.

Happy in your own mind that the stigma is in perfect condition, the pollen from the other parent can be applied; this can be administered in several ways. One method, using tweezers only, is to place onto the stigma the yellow head of the other flower from your second parent; with careful manipulation this

round varieties or two plum types, at least the fixing of the shape is not a problem, and more consideration can be given to the flavour and, most importantly, the resistance to disease. All the seedlings from the cross made will give a different variation

is the best and surest way. It does require deft handling, however, and the clumsier person should perhaps try another way.

A second method is to tilt the pollen flower to face downwards, and place your fingernail close to the flower tip; then tap the flower with a finger on the other hand, and if the pollen is ripe and ready, a small portion will drop onto your finger nail. This can then easily be 'touched' onto the sticky stigma – and this is usually all that is required to complete the cross. Within a few days the ovary at the base of the stigma will show whether the cross has 'taken'. Both these methods can be repeated two days later, if only to secure the cross; – and always check that the pollen flower is fully ripe with pollen to begin with – a fully open flower is generally a good guide to the condition required.

The problem of labelling is a tricky one, especially if the same plant is to accommodate several crosses. One method is to use coloured cotton to tie on the stem of the little floret behind the tiny flower, a different colour relating to each different cross; the colour and the cross details can then be put on a label placed in the soil below. Within a few days it will become evident that the ovary, or young tomato, is developing to produce the wanted seed.

SEED COLLECTING

The fruit should remain on the vine until ripe – with strict instructions to the family to leave well alone! It is a good idea to leave your picked crosses on the shelf in the greenhouse until they are overripe, because the pulp then comes away from the seed much more cleanly. Wash pulp and seed in a fine mesh sieve under running water, moving the seeds around with the fingers and rubbing them against the sieve sides; this leaves the seed free of pulp, and perfect for the drying process. Drying is achieved by laying the wet seed on kitchen roll paper on a warm windowsill, and turning after a couple of hours – or sooner, if in a sunny position. Remove them before they become glued to the paper, then place in a paper bag for several days to dry off completely, when they can be placed in a plastic bag or envelope until sowing time.

SEED SOWING

The time of sowing is left entirely to the reader, because the earlier the start, the better the conditions. The method of germination described below is a well used one, but extremely successful. For a small amount of seed, place a sheet of kitchen roll paper on a plate or similar container, cutting the paper to the roundness of the plate; lay the seeds on this, add water and then place a second sheet over the seeds, so enclosing them in a sandwich. Drain off the excess water. All that is then required is to place the plate plus seeds in a warm situation but not full sun, keeping the paper moist, but not wet – and 100 per cent germination can be expected. (This method is similar to sweet pea germination.) Sow the sprouting seeds in small, single pots with good seed compost in a warm position with full light: these conditions will bring along fine, healthy, stocky plants and your full germination.

F1 SEEDLINGS

The resulting seedlings will be the F1 generation, and all the plants so produced will be variable in some way from the parents. No two seedlings will be identical, but will show variations in one way or another; some will show outer signs not evident in the parents – the best will come finally in the tasting, which I can promise you will be a surprise.

Don't expect all the young plants to produce lovely sweet tomatoes – far from it, and some will enter the waste bin as soon as the first bite is taken. But keep cheerful, because one on two will possess that special something that the palette will adore, and these are the ones to back-cross to the better flavoured parent. Although the special newcomer has the flavour you like, the resulting seeds saved from it will not produce all the same plants in the F2 generation, the reason being, that at this stage the plants are not fixed. This means that the seedlings in the F2 will show variations in all genetic departments, including the flavour. It is from the new seedlings that another tasting will be compared to the favoured F1 and when found, seed from this F2 will be saved to produce the F3.

This process is the way to fix any characteristics that you would like to be permanent, at the same time carefully discarding any undesirable features present in the seedlings. Sometimes these plants are fixed in a couple of generations, then again, many may take longer.

Finally, when the plant has been found that meets your satisfaction and the seedling is at last fixed, you

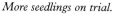

More seedlings on trial.

ABOVE: *Young tomato fruit ripening.*

RIGHT: *Two seedlings from the same fruit showing quite a colour difference.*

Healthy truss from new seedling.

can save all the seeds your require, knowing full well that all the future plants will be identical in all departments, including the flavour. Now all that remains to do is to decide a name for your very own tomato with the flavour like no other.

The reason for back-crossing to the best parent is to bring the better qualities of the parent into the next generation; this promises a better line of attack than saving seed direct from a mediocre seedling. This method does throw the genes and chromosomes from both plants into the mixing pot, but at least you know that some of the finer qualities are in abundance, and the chances or producing first class seedlings are higher, thus giving the fixing process something special to work on.

More seedlings on trial.

Strawberries

SIMPLICITY GUIDE

Measure of difficulty	Crossing stage	Flower to seed	Seed germination	Seedling stage
FAIRLY EASY	FAIRLY EASY	EASY	EASY	EASY

SITES FOR BEST RESULTS Open, sunny position required. Not too near trees. Rich, well drained soil.
SPECIAL NOTES Plant in late July to give the young plants a good period of time to build good fruiting crowns before the winter sets in.

The smell of strawberries fresh from the garden is deliciously mouthwatering. When picked just moments before, the fruit has that ambrosial flavour that only a home-grown strawberry can possess – and how much more gratifying when the fruits are a direct result of one of your very own varieties. And it is quite easy to achieve this satisfying position if you follow the methods detailed below.

Many years ago the only types available were the wild *Fragaria vesca* (wood strawberry) and *Fragaria elatior* (hautbois strawberry), and although on the small side, their sweetness made them firm favourites at harvest time. By the seventeenth century the North American Strawberry (*virginiana*) had been introduced, and later, in the eighteenth century, the Chilean strawberry (*Fragaria chiloensis*), which bears large, purplish fruits, was brought into Europe via France. They naturally crossed with the wild varieties, producing seedling bearing the qualities of both parents.

Later, by the nineteenth century, new varieties were introduced by way of 'Keen's Seedling' in 1821, and the famous Laxton's Royal Sovereign in 1892, and these are still going strong. These were the beginnings of the lovely fruit we take for granted, and for which we can find so many wonderful varieties today, all descendants of the wild, sweet species developed by the careful manipulation of the plant breeder and with the co-operation of Mother Nature.

It is advisable to start with the finest varieties of plants that are available; this will secure a foundation for quality stock essential to the breeding

A typical flower.

programme. Two plants, each of a different variety, are needed to produce something new, although to venture into line breeding or crossbreeding, three or four varieties make for fascinating experiments. When selecting the initial stock, go to a specialist nursery, not only to have the widest choice possible, but to secure disease-free plants: this should ensure a flying start. The modern varieties grown by the specialists are certified disease free, and this is a very important factor, since any virus in the initial stock will ruin the whole crop. You must also decide what type of plant you intend to develop, whether you want a small or a tall plant, big berries, or early or late varieties. These are the 'ground rules': keep them in view and they will guide you to your ultimate purpose, and save you breeding too much second-rate stock.

An ideal time to purchase the stock plants – in this case I suggest new runners – is July, if possible. A newly potted, healthy-looking runner can be fed with a general liquid feed for a month, before being finally planted into its permanent position in early August. The final ground must be well nourished before planting, although feeding with potash in September will harden the plants and help them survive the winter weather. By the time October is upon us, the runners will be well grown and hardy, and if things have gone according to plan, will be showing signs of a plump heart, the flower buds for the following May. I know of one top class commercial grower who trims down the crowns to a single one to each plant, cutting out the others, and he maintains that all the fruits produced are large and luscious, with the same wonderful flavour and no tiny stragglers. I believe him, but I have not had the courage to copy him.

In the spring, as soon as the plants show signs of awakening, feed with potash only. Many growers feed nitrogen to give the plants a spurt, but this gives luscious leaves with much of the heart being wasted on greenery, whereas feeding potash produces an abundance of flowers, each one of which will produce the treasured fruit. If the plants are to be grown on for another season, then give a general feed as soon as the cropping season ends, as this will build up the vigour and stamina of the plant; also cut off all the runners not required as early as possible.

THE CROSS

Before the crossing of the two varieties can be accomplished both plants must be in flower; this will be some time in May, though naturally this depends on the location. The flower to be the seed parent must be operated on first: choose one that is still in the bud stage, and open it up carefully with tweezers, first taking off the petals, then plucking out all the stamens, leaving the yellow mound still untouched with pollen; also take a closer look at the stigmatic parts to make sure that no pollen has been shed, and if you are in any doubt about this, use another unopened bud.

Cover the exposed flower with a paper bag to prevent insects from trespassing, and leave overnight. By lunchtime next day, take a fully open flower from the male plant and apply pollen by dusting the flower head onto the female stigmas. This procedure can be repeated the following day, and the day after if time permits – this operation is so important that an extra day would certainly be well worth while. Several applications of pollen will prevent malformed fruits, which are usually caused by poor pollination. Cover again with the bag to keep out the opposition until the strawberry can be seen starting to form; at this point the bag can be removed to allow the berry to form to its natural size. Obviously if this pollinating

The ideal flower bud to use in the cross.

Petals taken off showing the stigma and stamens.

The stamens are removed leaving stamens ready to pollinate.

performance can be accomplished in a greenhouse, or indeed indoors, there is no need for the bag. This is an ideal method if only one or two crosses are intended, and the plants are grown in pots.

Record all the crosses made, and mark the plants at the time of pollination; it is very easy to forget which was which as picking time approaches. When making crosses with plants, always write the female parent first – the seed parent – then the male, pollen parent: this pedigree will be very helpful in planning further developments. Guard the developing fruit not only from the birds, mice or slugs, but from the family, who no doubt will never notice the labels tied to your precious fruits.

As the berry begins to colour, place the pollinated one into a jam jar, but still attached to the plant, to protect it from the birds. If the jar is tilted to the plant, with the base slightly higher than the open end, no rain can get into it to damage the fruit; this berry can then be allowed to stay on the plant longer than usual to ripen fully, making for easier seed collection.

SEED COLLECTION

Leave the berry on the plant until it is slightly over-ripe; even if it is left until it is soft, no harm will come to it. Removing the seed is an easy task, since it is on the outer surface of the fruit and not inside,

Seeds on the outside of the fruit.

as with blackberries or raspberries. Place the seeds in a tea strainer and rinse under gently running water; this will remove any fruit pulp still adhering to them, especially if stirred with a finger – but make sure they stay in the strainer and don't go over the edge and down the sink – it happens to us all. Rinsing the fruit is important to eradicate any chance of disease from the pulp left on the seed.

Dry the seed on a sheet of kitchen paper, and you are ready for the next step: this can mean saving until the spring, or sowing immediately. Seed will keep

The ripe fruit with seeds ready to be removed and washed.

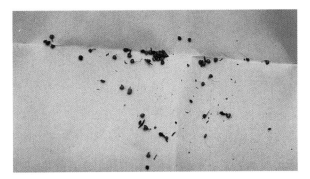

Seeds taken from the fruit ready to sow.

Seedlings ready to be transplanted.

when well dried and placed in an airtight container. If you are considering sowing the seed as soon as it is ripe, good germination should be the result, though bear in mind that any developing seedling will most likely require some sort of protection during the first winter; a cold greenhouse would be ideal, although a cold frame will suffice. The advantage of this early sowing is that the plant is a good size by the time spring arrives, giving it a flying start and consolidating its growth and a good root system ready for planting out in August. If, on the other hand, a spring sowing is preferred, an early start will help to produce the perfect plant for autumn planting. It is worth mentioning here that some seedlings when they first appear from germination don't look like strawberries, but can look very much like weeds, not always showing the usual strawberry leaf, but round and non-serrated ones; some seedlings can get to four leaves before the characteristic strawberry shape appears, so don't discard anything until you are absolutely certain what it is.

Strawberry seedlings grow well in both soil-based and soil-less composts, but there is one important point to be made regarding soil-less compost: if sown in this sort of compost, when plated out into the garden soil, the plant roots seem reluctant to enter the soil from their own rootball. If, on the other hand, some soil-less compost is mixed into the planting hole with the garden soil, much better results will be achieved. When soil compost is used initially this problem does not arise. This method can cater for any compost used.

Once away, the little plants grow rapidly and should develop quite a decent heart by the time planting out time arrives. If an early start was made and the plants are of a good size by August, a crop could be expected the following year, good enough to assist in the selection of the better seedlings to keep. Make a provisional selection from the first batch, taking into consideration all the factors required from a first-class fruit. Surprises can be expected: not all the fruits will be so tasty for one thing, and the sizes of the flowers will most likely differ, as will the petal count. All manner of characteristics could be

Trials to test for potential new varieties.

apparent, but we are looking for a plant that is better than the parents used, and that possesses all the requirements of the family.

Records must be kept and plants marked, with their characteristics noted. A selection of the best plants can be earmarked for further trialling. During the time the plants were producing their fruits, stolons were growing from the crown of the plant; these will produce the runners required for further testing. As they develop, the runners can be placed onto a pot of good compost, and a loop of wire pushed in to hold the plantling in place until a good root system is formed; then sever it from the main plant. After the test runners are taken, cut off any others from the main plant, as this must have its second year to prove its worth; a good general fertilizer will fortify it for the test the following year.

Six runners from each of the selected plants will give the best trial for the final selection; if these are planted into good, prepared ground as soon as they are severed from the mother plant, they will develop the huge heart necessary to mature the plant to its full potential. Feeding will help to build up the heart, although if the ground was in a good fertile condition from the start, no other food will be necessary until mid-September when a potash feed, as stated before, will harden the plants for the winter.

WHAT NEXT?

Now that you are in possession of your very own variety of strawberry, try to produce something better by going through the same exercise again, by back-crossing your variety to the best parent or crossing with a sister seedling. These methods will bring more recessive genes, which could in fact supply more fascinating plants than those already on hand.

Soft Fruits

Measure of difficulty	Crossing stage	Flower to seed	Seed germination	Seedling stage
DIFFICULT	DIFFICULT	EASY	NOT EASY	EASY

SITES FOR BEST RESULTS Deep, rich ground in full sun is ideal, then trained along a fence or wires does produce perfect fruits – but we all know that the plants will make a show in any position. The better the conditions, the better the produce.

SPECIAL NOTES Precise crossing procedures must be followed to be certain that the seedlings are from the intended cross and not an insect cross.

The soft fruit title covers a vast range of selective varieties, ranging from the wild type of brambles to the more sophisticated hybrids that are blendings of many well known species. They all fall into the various categories that come into the province of the hybridist, and will fulfil the demands of the most adventurous; moreover all the different varieties can be manipulated, and some wonderful hybrids can be achieved with varying tastes and even berry types. The majority of the offspring will be lacking in quality, as can be expected, but be assured that some very good seedlings of a unique nature can, and will, put in an appearance, and every one of the seedlings will show some dissimilarity to the next, even from other seedlings grown from the same berry fruit.

BLACKBERRIES AND RASPBERRIES

These two berries are the most popular species grown by the average gardener, and the methods used for these in the breeding programme can be applied to all the other soft fruits. Crossbreeding two different blackberries will give the expected blackberry of a type, but the majority will be nondescript, although some varying flavours can be forthcoming from one or two which could supply

Raspberry seedlings making good progress.

a wonderful flavour to your liking. There are some very sophisticated types of blackberry and raspberry crossed varieties, and practically every one has been produced in this crossbreeding method; crossing blackberry into raspberry will be a hybrid

Seedlings growing on in pots.

BELOW: *Young seedlings prior to planting out.*

that can be completely different from either of the two parents, and with a very wide range of flavours ranging from fairly sweet to downright bitter – but also some very palatable fruits to tantalize the taste buds.

Exciting blendings of the contrasting fruits can be achieved, and it is not too long to wait for the final results to be analysed in the fruit bowls on the kitchen table. Some of the popular hybrid crosses between the blackberry and raspberry already on the market are varieties such as 'Sunberry', 'Tayberry', 'Veitchberry' and 'King's Acre', all giving their own identity in the way of shape, style, colour and flavour, not to mention leaf and growth characteristics.

MORE HYBRIDS

Venturing into the hybrid field can be quite an experience, and there may be some fine-looking plants amongst the seedlings. All hybrids are the result of crosses previously created, and these can be incorporated into more crosses with either species or other hybrids, with the aim of producing a unique seedling.

THE CROSS

It is recognized that when crossing two different fruits, it is the seed parent that will stamp the offspring, so the seedlings will eventually look like that type of plant; so to achieve the type required, it would help to use that same type as the seed parent. This is not a sound ruling, but merely a guideline, as I have produced plants that look nothing

The seedlings will bloom and fruit next season.

BELOW: *Seedlings growing from seed the first year will flower the next year.*

BELOW RIGHT: *A typical soft fruit flower.*

like either parent and have been more vigorous than both, which proves that there are still more wonderful varieties to be developed.

When selection of the parents is finalized, find a bud as usual showing colour but still tightly closed, gently remove the petals and stamens – it's a small flower, so be extra careful – leaving the mound of stigmas in the centre in immaculate condition. With the magnifying glass, examine the mound of stigmas very closely; I use a watchmaker's eye glass, which gives a clear view of all of them, so you are absolutely sure that no pollen has alighted on them before your own is applied. Cover with a paper bag in case of intrusion until the following day; then examine them with the magnifying glass, and as long as the tips of the stigmas glisten, showing that the pollen is acceptable, the cross can be made. To do this, find a fully open flower from the proposed male plant which shows plenty of pollen, and gently brush the flower head onto the stigmas; repeat this a couple of times, and a successful result will be guaranteed – and don't forget the marking procedure.

The ideal buds to be emasculated, the largest of the bunch.

Only the stigma remains, the stamens are removed and it is now ready for pollen.

Crossed flower showing the development of the fruit. Tag attached.

The crossed flower developing fruit. Note the opposition.

THE SEEDS

When the resulting berries are ripe, pick them and place them on a saucer to ripen fully; you can even let them go mushy and overripe. Then place them on a piece of kitchen paper, and press them into the paper with the fingers to remove the juices and the pulp; the seeds can be put into a tea strainer and washed in the usual way to clean off every particle of fruit until they are lovely and clean. Make sure the strainer has a small enough mesh not to let any seeds through it, and as an extra precaution, place the plug in the sink in case some escape. The seeds are hard and tough, so the finger treatment will not do them any harm. In fact, this will help towards removing any inhibitors present in the seed coating.

SEED SOWING

The seed of most soft fruits, as with hard fruits, requires a period of cold treatment before germination can take place; this can be achieved by sowing it in sterilized moist compost, covering the pot with glass or clingfilm – to protect it from insects, mice and birds – and then leaving it outside to take the full brunt of the winter. If a small mesh wire is used to cover the pot, so much the better, as the rain passing through the pot will help to break down the inhibitors in the seed coating, which prevents premature germination. Always keep an eye on the seed during the winter in case any seedlings appear very early, which often happens.

When the spring arrives, place them in a warm position, and some of the seeds should germinate. They are quite notorious for being reluctant to appear, and sometimes take two seasons before they do so – and once they do appear, they are slow to get going; but then all of a sudden they will reach for the sky in a powerful surge. This is the first long vine, which is next year's first fruiting stem.

A second method of treatment for soft fruit seed is the same as that for the apple or pear, which is to place the seed with damp vermiculite in a plastic bag. Then place the package in the salad compartment of the refrigerator, and leave it there until the spring. It is essential that the soil used in the pots is sterilized because of the time the seed spends in the soil, and its need to be protected from fungal disease and soil disorders.

The following spring will see new side growths spreading out from the long vine, which will supply the fruits during the summer months. When the first season's fruits are collected, they may be analysed as to quality in all departments – and believe me, they will be varied!

SELECTION

Once the mixed seedlings have fruited, an assessment can be made as to which vines are the better flavoured and the better looking, the leaf characteristics and so on, and a final choice made as to which will be your number one selection. This plant is then grown on for another year to allow it to attain its true fruit size and vigour; it needs all of this time to produce its best crop in order for you to give it a final assessment.

The trend today is for thornless varieties, but when using these in a cross with thorny types, the thorny types are more dominant; some thornless ones may appear, but they lack vigour in the first cross. The way to overcome this dilemma is to back-cross the best seedling, thornless or not, to the best thornless parent, and this cross will give a small percentage of thornless vines with better vigour and which are more often stronger plants. This applies only if you used at least one thornless variety in the first cross.

The next step is to save one of the berries from your best seedling plant, and repeat the process of producing the next F2 generation, this will give a further selection, and this time probably showing the qualities of a better plant because you are selecting from the best produced. From this F2 generation batch of seedlings will emerge a mixed variation, but when the final selection is made, this plant should show some of the qualities we have been looking for. By the time the seedling chosen in the F2 generation showing good characteristics has passed through two generations and still possesses the attributes required, then we are dealing with a first-class plant that will be capable of passing on its supreme traits to successive generations of seedlings if selfed. Any outcrossing to this seedling will start the process of selection all over again.

It will not be an easy ride, because the larger, sweeter berries are reluctant to appear, and large-berried parents are the ones to use in order to attain this goal. Sweetness varies in every vine, so that department should first occupy the breeder; and once a sweet type is produced, try to use this vine as you endeavour to develop the size – and eventually it is to be hoped that the large, sweet berry will grace your fruit bowl.

All the soft fruits can be tried in the breeding programme, but a good record of plants crossed is essential to trace the different pedigrees so that back-crossing can be applied to double up on special features, at the same time avoiding any failed or impoverished results. Selecting and using only top-quality seedlings that possess the attributes required is the best step forward.

Heathland Berries

SIMPLICITY GUIDE

Measure of difficulty	Crossing stage	Flower to seed	Seed germination	Seedling stage
DIFFICULT	DIFFICULT	EASY	EXPERIENCE	FAIRLY EASY

SITES FOR BEST RESULTS The most important factor with these plants is the need to have acid conditions. If camellias or rhododendrons grow in your soil, then these plants will flourish.

SPECIAL NOTES Use boiled, cooled rainwater at every stage of watering, and only ericaceous soil for sowing and re-potting the seedlings.

BLUEBERRIES AND CRANBERRIES

Both these berries can be self-crossed to provide a variation in fruit, although they are not so popular in the UK as in other countries, especially the United States, where they are becoming more popular than ever before. The main reason for failure in the UK is the lack of knowledge regarding the conditions that are needed to produce a healthy plant capable of supplying a bumper crop: in one word, acidity. They are acid-loving plants and will not tolerate any other condition; if rhododendrons, azaleas and camellias grow well in your garden, then these berries will flourish.

When watering plants, one important factor overlooked by many people, even though they realize the importance of using acid soil, is that tap water nearly always contains lime, a killer to heathberries and the shrubs mentioned above. Therefore use only rainwater, with an occasional dose of the fertilizer Sequestrene: this helps to release, amongst other minerals, the iron that is sometimes locked in acid soil and is unavailable to plants, but is accessible after the application.

Crossing these plants involves an identical procedure to dealing with raspberries and blackberries, and providing the acid soil conditions are observed, then good results and excellent cross-breeding should offer most outstanding fruits. When potting up these acid-loving plants to use as parents in the greenhouse, use only ericaceous compost with rainwater; the results will be worth all the trouble taken.

Red-, Black- and Whitecurrants, and Gooseberries

SIMPLICITY GUIDE

Measure of difficulty	Crossing stage	Flower to seed	Seed germination	Seedling stage
VERY DIFFICULT	TRICKY	FAIRLY EASY	EXPERIENCE	FAIRLY EASY

SITES FOR BEST RESULTS Neutral soil.
SPECIAL NOTES Flowers are so tiny that special care is needed.

These plants can be crossed, and various results expected, but the only drawback is the size of the flowers, which are so small that a magnifying glass is needed to confirm the pureness of the cross. The bud has to be emasculated (petals and stamens removed) before the stamens are ripe with pollen, and before the insect world decides to interfere. By using the magnifying glass, the flower can be seen in all its splendour, and the items removed much more easily. A needle can be used to prize away the stamens from the circle around the stigma, though be warned that through the glass the needle looks

Open flowers showing the stigma and stamens.

Use the closed young flowers for the seed parent.

Bushes of healthy flowers showing stamens ripe with pollen.

BELOW LEFT: *Fruits growing from the two crossed flowers.*

BELOW: *Ripe seed taken fresh from the redcurrant berry.*

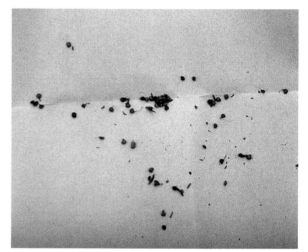

more like a broom handle! However, once a few flowers have been attempted you will manage this procedure quite easily without the magnifying glass, although it is essential to check the pureness of the stigma tip with it.

The procedure regarding pollination is similar to all other flowers with a lone stigma in the centre, namely when it is ready, touch it very gently with a single stamen taken from an open flower of the

A typical gooseberry flower.

The ideal bud to emasculate and remove stamens.

ABOVE LEFT: *Flower with ripe stamens full of pollen.*

LEFT: *Flower showing immature stamens. Young stigma in the centre.*

ABOVE: *This is a cross between a gooseberry and a blackcurrant.*

other variety. This calls for precision, and can only be accomplished by a very steady hand. The result will be another berry, but this special will hold the genetic selections of your own choosing. When ripe, the berry can have exactly the same treatment as the blackberry above, and the seeds should be treated in the same way, with the cold treatment as well.

The resulting plants will give fruit the second year when you will be able to analyse the findings and also select further crosses to be made.

Hard Fruits

SIMPLICITY GUIDE

Measure of difficulty	Crossing stage	Flower to seed	Seed germination	Seedling stage
FAIRLY EASY	FAIRLY EASY	EASY	FAIRLY EASY	EASY

SITES FOR BEST RESULTS Most fruit trees grow best in open spaces in good, well drained land, but if used for dwarfing trees, then large pots are useful. Feed well.

SPECIAL NOTES Seedlings grow better and fruit quicker when they are grafted onto dwarfing stock; this makes it easier to train them and to control any problems with disease.

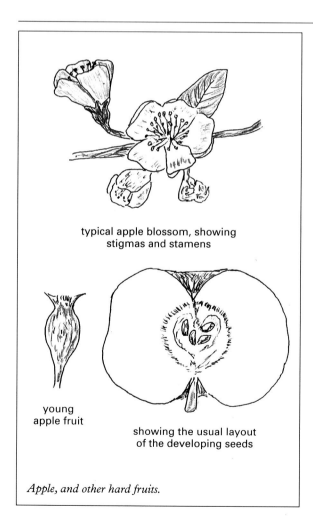

typical apple blossom, showing
stigmas and stamens

young
apple fruit

showing the usual layout
of the developing seeds

Apple, and other hard fruits.

APPLES

Although it is fairly simple to cross-fertilize your own fruit trees, the drawback is the length of time you must wait for the young plants to bear fruit. Sometimes an incredible seven years can elapse before the first fruit is obtainable, so this area of breeding is not for the impatient hybridist. Many of the fruits will oblige in a shorter time, but nothing

A typical apple blossom.

is quick to produce; nevertheless there are plenty of details to follow to keep the project interesting, and certain exciting times will be evident along the way. Also, most hard fruits require another pollinator to secure an abundance of fruit, although this will become an asset to the breeding programme.

Other varieties of fruit can be treated in exactly the same way as the apple, which is discussed here, although any varying methods will be highlighted at the required time. Any apple picked from the tree and the seed content planted will generally produce a fruit tree of some kind, but the fruits will include a very high percentage of nondescript specimens, and to wait seven years for a third-rate tree to emerge is indeed a serious waste of time. Rather than take this path of uncertainty, it is surely worth the extra effort to follow a planned programme in the hope of some kind of success, even though the same uninspiring results could be the end result. Many of the new varieties have appeared this way, although most have been the product of planned development.

Parent Selection

Select a young tree still in a pot or container of the variety chosen as the prospective seed bearer; having it in its pot is a great advantage in that it can be placed in a position safe from insects during that vital time when cross-pollination is imminent. It can be grown completely outside until the time the cross is made – in fact the development of the young tree must be continued in its normal hardy conditions, and it should be taken into an insect-free area for only the shortest period whilst the cross is in progress.

The time to isolate the young tree and prepare for the emasculation of the flower is when it is in the closed bud stage. As usual, take off the plant's stamens before any pollen can alight on its own stigma; although most fruit trees are self-sterile, this precaution is taken because there are some varieties that have been introduced that are self-compatible, and if they self-pollinated this would spoil the intended cross. Open the closed bud by plucking off the petals, and take out the whole outer ring of immature stamens until only the stigmas are left. At this stage the stigmas are also immature, and can be left until the next day or the day after to develop a ripe condition; in their protected situation

The ideal buds to select for cross-pollination.

Selected bud opened showing the stamens to be removed.

Stamens removed. Stigma ready for selected pollen.

Starting the development of the fruit.

they will be safe from marauding insects with their unwanted pollen.

When the stigmas are ripe, as shown by the sticky surface to the tops, the pollen from the selected male parent can be applied; this is best done by taking a fully open flower from the male tree and gently dusting the stigma tips with the stamens coated in pollen – the same procedure as with the soft fruits. Tie on the label showing the cross varieties and the date. A second application of pollen would be wise to ensure a good covering; several different flowers from the male plant can be dusted onto the stigmas. Be very careful to do this with the gentlest of touches, because if the stigmas are damaged they will be useless.

Leave the young plant in its safe situation for a few days to ensure that the cross is a success, and then the plant can be grown on in the normal way to develop its fruit. Leave the fruit until it is fully ripe, and protect it not only from the birds, wasps and the like but also from the family.

The Seed

When the ripe fruit is picked, place it in a position when it will become thoroughly overripe, until the flesh is very soft and almost unpalatable; at this stage press out the seeds, which by now will be fully developed. Wash all the pulp away and place the seed in a glass of warm water for several days, changing the water on each day; you will notice that the water will have a slight brown colour, due to the dissolving of some of the inhibitors present in the seed. These prevent early germination, and it is an advantage to

wash them away. After several of these soakings the seed can be placed with a handful of damp vermiculite into a plastic bag, which should be sealed with the label enclosed; then place it in the salad compartment of the refrigerator for at least two months.

After this period the seed can be sown in a pot of good seed compost and placed in a propagator or on the windowsill to germinate. Watch out for early germination during the cold spell in the salad compartment, as several may show shoots after a short period. These can be sown to get an early start, and the remainder replaced to complete the cold spell; also some seeds will germinate direct from the fruit to the seed compost, although a better percentage will be from the cold process.

When the seedlings are growing well it will be wise to graft them onto dwarfing stock, because they will then have the benefit of a strong, mature root system, and this will bring the seedling into fruition in two to three years instead of the seven if left on its own roots. The other benefit provided by the stock plant is the chance to grow the type of fruit tree required; thus a dwarf stock will keep your new seedling to the size selected or intermediate, whichever is preferred. Naturally if the new seedling is grown to maturity on its own root system it will almost inevitably grow to a very large, tall tree and

The seedlings germinating.

Seedlings ready to be grafted onto dwarfing apple stock.

In the spring, cut back the stock just above the graft.

will not fruit until a few years later; so the advantage in grafting is quite considerable.

Selection

The young plants will grow at quite a fast pace, and will provide some handsome buds to apply to the root stock in the summer; but if left for the full season they will have one or two stems which could make good scions to be grafted in the late winter or early the following spring.

The next step will be ensuring a healthy plant until fruiting time, when the fruits can be picked and assessed as to the quality for your own palate. Remember, every seed sown will produce a fruit completely different from all others, so your fruit will be unique and will perhaps provide the type of fruit you have always looked for. If you keep a good record of the crosses made, then at least back-crosses can be attempted to a parent plant in the hope of highlighting the best of both worlds. Most new fruit orchards are grafted onto dwarfing stocks because it is that much easier to care for them: the full tree can be sprayed without difficulty, pruning is simpler, and even if the fruit quantity is lower, the overall quality is unsurpassed – all of which saves immensely on manpower.

The main stocks used for apples are as follows: M27 'extremely dwarfing', ideal for cordons or containers and can fruit in two years; M9 'very dwarfing' though it still needs staking and requires plenty of feeding, and it is advisable to plant in good soil; and M26, which is a more vigorous stock, and one that I recommend because it can fruit in three years and will supply more fruit than the M9.

At this stage, remember that most hard fruits require a different variety to pollinate the blossom, so if the grafted seedlings are grown in containers, place them in the vicinity of another variety to ensure good pollination.

OTHER FRUITS

The same crossbreeding system can be applied to most hard fruits, although the dwarfing stock for grafting will be different for every type of fruit; the ones above are for apples. Pears will require a quince stock, usually quince A or a quince C, but this is only slightly more dwarfing. They also require a pollinator variety, although there are some self-fertile varieties appearing in the catalogues.

Rootstocks for plums and gages are most widely grown on St Julien A, but the new Pixie stock is becoming more popular and more dwarfing.

Cherries can be treated in the same manner, and they are grafted onto the new type Colt, which is still on the large size but much more dwarf than the plant's own root system.

Another good stock from Belgium is the GM9; some of the self-fertile Stella variety can be bought at the garden centres.

All the above plants, unless of a self-fertile variety, will require the services of another variety to ensure good pollination.

Vegetables

Measure of difficulty	Crossing stage	Flower to seed	Seed germination	Seedling stage
CAN BE DIFFICULT	CAN BE DIFFICULT	EASY	EASY	EASY

SITES FOR BEST RESULTS A good allotment is perfect. Good fertile soil will produce wonderful crops.

SPECIAL NOTES Most vegetables are difficult to cross, although once mastered, everything is simple. Taking note of the perfect timing will produce your own flavour of produce.

FRENCH BEANS

The French bean has been used as a source of nutrition for many thousands of years with their delicate, stringless, succulent pods. The family of beans, including runner beans, pole beans and many other variations, first originated in South America in the countries of Mexico, Bolivia, Guatemala, Peru and even Argentina. The wild varieties have grown for centuries in the high mountains of these countries, in cool damp undergrowths or low-lying shrubberies, which provided an ideal environment for their trailing habit.

It is assumed that they were more domesticated in these areas, and that better varieties were developed by the selection of the best by the local people: as the better beans were always saved, the successive crops showed a steady improvement. It wasn't until the time of the Spanish domination of this continent that these beans were introduced into Europe, but they have developed very quickly so that today we enjoy several varieties. This means the hybridizer need only manipulate the existing ones to perfect his very own variety.

Selection

There are so many kinds of bean from which to select two parents to create a new variation; a quick look through the seed catalogues will give an idea of the broad range of beans available. French beans are the short ones, and the tall ones are called pole varieties, but they all belong to the same family *Phaseolus vulgaris*. Included in the family are kidney beans and haricots, and all can be used to produce something new. The fact that they are self-pollinating is very helpful, and will make life much simpler for the breeding programme.

The colours alone have a wide spectrum, ranging from the darkest greens through blue, purple, yellow and even red striped. Only be careful when selection is made because some beans are grown for the seed alone, whereas others as the French bean, are a cultured pod type. Attempt a cross with whichever takes your fancy, and you may produce something we have never seen – although almost certainly somewhere along the line it will have been attempted.

The beginner would be advised to start with just two plants, one of each variety, and grown in pots so that isolating them will be an easy matter later; it also means you have better management control over each plant as the period of crossing approaches. The seed can be sown early in the season in a warm greenhouse or on a windowsill, but they must be hardened off before standing outside, when they will achieve their natural development.

The Cross

Once the plants are growing strongly and beginning to show flower, take them back into the greenhouse or onto the windowsill, and let the first few flowers develop and show signs of setting seed without any help from you. This is because the French bean and all varieties of the pea and bean families have a natural habit to bud drop at an early stage; but after the first two or three flowers, the plants settle down and produce their fruits.

To perform the cross, select an unopened bud and continue the exact procedure, as explained in the sweet pea chapter. Cover the flower bud to prevent any interference, and allow to complete to the fertilizing stage. The method is almost exactly the same as that used for the sweet pea, which will show the same type of bud formation protecting the special seed created from the cross. Once the pods are forming, it will be better to care for the plants outside in the open, though make sure the pedigree labels are in position as soon as the cross has been made. A reciprocal cross can be made to reverse the cross using the same procedure, but one each way is usually enough, as too many seeds all giving a slightly different gene combination will only lead to confusion when analysing the final results.

If more than one cross was made, keep each cross result separate, as each will have a difference in texture as well as a possible variation in taste. Furthermore these need to be grown separately the following season so that personal tasting can be carried out by the family, and the selected bean produced to supply beans for successive seasons on a permanent basis.

LETTUCE

The garden lettuce, as it is now known, is thought to have been developed from the prickly lettuce, and has been grown throughout Europe and northern America for as long as records began. However, today's lettuce is far removed from its prickly parent forefathers, and has developed from the single type, loose-leaf wild plant to a family that varies widely, from butterhead, cos and crispy iceberg to the loose-leaf salad bowl type; there is also a wide variation in colour. The fact that the species inbreeds naturally makes it a perfect subject with which to develop your very own variety.

Most good gardeners have probably never seen a lettuce in flower, firstly because the plants are used

before they bolt, or because they are pulled up for the compost heap when they blow. Nevertheless, the two different varieties selected to supply the new generation will have to be grown near to each other for convenience, or potted up and grown to maturity. The plants will flower after the mature plants have blown – or 'gone over', as some gardeners say – but must be left to throw up the flower stalk. This is a critical time, and to prevent the heart from rotting before the flower has fully developed, it is advisable to remove most of the leaves around the base.

The Flower

Of all the plants discussed so far, the lettuce is by far the most complicated to crossbreed because the flower is ripe for only a few hours before pollination takes place. The flower has up to twenty-four florets, each with its own ovary, from which grows the stigma surrounded by five anthers joined as a tube. The ripening of the pollen coincides with the elongation of the stigma, which grows through the five pollen stamens, so self-fertilizing with its own pollen.

The skill is to take away the stamens before the pollen is ripe without causing damage to the stigma; you can then apply pollen from your other selected variety. To do this you will need a good magnifying glass plus a very steady hand. The professional way is to be ready early enough to see the flower opening, then to apply a fine jet of water into the floret to wash out all the pollen as it ripens, leaving the stigma wet but undamaged. If it dries quickly, the stigma can be pollinated from the other selected plant; this operation takes place as the floret opens, but must be completed before it closes, never to open again until the seed is set. Keep a watch on the stamens, as they don't all ripen at the precise time and some can ripen after your selected pollen has been placed, only to spoil your cross. If this approach were tried using two different types or colours, the results would prove that you were successful (or not).

It does sound complicated, and it is, but it will be worth the trouble when your new variety is on the family table. When the masterpiece has arrived, all that is required is to allow some plants to set seed; these should be identical to your own grown variety.

SHRUBS

Measure of difficulty	Crossing stage	Flower to seed	Seed germination	Seedling stage
CAN BE TRICKY	CAN BE TRICKY	USUALLY EASY	EXPERIENCE	FAIRLY EASY

SITES FOR BEST RESULTS Most shrubs will grow almost anywhere, but each species must be treated according to that particular variety. Good fertile soil will benefit all of them.

SPECIAL NOTES When treating pure species, then very little variation will occur. Hybrid shrubs will produce a variation of plants and these will give the grower more pleasure.

Shrubs of all kinds can be manipulated by the hybridist, and new variations can easily be produced with little trouble. Just look at the colour mixture of plants such as cotoneaster, pyracanthas, potentillas, lilac (syringa), buddleia and berberis, to name just a few – and this is not just the delightful variation of coloured flowers, but the flamboyant berry harvest, too. By crossing two different coloured berry pyracantha varieties, they will produce the colour berries most similar to the seed parent, but by taking the F2 generation, a mixture of colours will be amongst the seedlings. Each coloured plant can be propagated by cuttings to produce enough plants of the colour required to supply the needs of the grower. The seeds produced from these plants require a cold spell before good germination can be expected, but by using the same procedure as for apples or roses, an excellent germination can be expected.

Berberis in all its varieties can produce the same results, giving the excitement of blending the coloured leaf varieties with plants possessing wonderful coloured flowers, besides the different hues of the fruits. The berberis fruits will usually contain two seeds which are easily parted from the pulp; wash and soak these in warm water for a day or two before planting them in sterilized compost, then place the pots in a cold frame ready for a spring germination. Some berberis seed will germinate without the cold spell, but a larger percentage of seedlings results from the cold spell method. As the seed emerges, either

spray or water with a fungicide to protect from damping off disease whilst the seedlings are at a vulnerable stage; once the seedlings are growing well, they become very resistant to most ailments.

The lilac (syringa) will produce some lovely variations. There is a lovely large lilac tree in a garden a few miles away from my house, which every spring cascades its lovely racemes of deep blue flowers. I admired it on many occasions in passing, and then one day I saw lots of seedpods hanging on the tree; this was now mid-winter, and the seed must have stood some very cold winds, rain and frost. I asked the occupant of the property if he would allow me to take some to try to germinate them, and he agreed. I sowed the seed immediately and placed it in a propagator at 18°C (65°F), and in less than a month, 50 per cent of the seed germinated, with others emerging later. The stratification period must have taken place on the tree in the cold winter weather. The results were varied indeed, with many different shades of blue, from sky blue to deep blue to almost purple, as well as one white; at least half were worth growing on, whilst some were very robust plants even though lacking beauty in the flowers. The owner of the original tree was amazed that the lovely plants I returned to him had been produced from the specimen he grew. The fact that his tree was a hybrid resulted in the variation in the progeny. It must be realized that most seedlings from such an experiment will be sub-standard if

Buds in an ideal stage to emasculate.

Removing the stamens with tweezers.

Stamens to be removed before they ripen.

the assistance of the breeder's imagination and skills in manipulating the intricacies of cross-pollination. Many untried combinations have still to be found, and treading the path that no one else has tried is the only way to reach something never seen before.

Once something new has been proven as to healthy growth and disease-free capabilities, and is good enough to warrant popular demand, then this becomes a very valuable asset, and one the creator should certainly be proud of.

The stamens removed.

compared to the mother tree, but some very worthy seedlings can also appear.

Even the softer shrubs such as the lavateras, abutilons, hibiscus and potentilla are all capable of producing different colours, and many of the tender plant seeds will germinate without the cold spell; though some are better with this addition. Almost every living plant can be encouraged to change with

INDEX

References to illustrations are shown in **bold** type.

african violets 16–19, **16–18**
  ericaceous compost 18
  growing the seed 18
  multiplying the stock 19
  potting on 19
  seedling care 19
  selecting 19
  temperature 18
  von Saint Paul, Baron Walter 16
aquilegia 20–3, **20–3**
  Aquilegia alpina 20
    jonesii 20
    longissima 20
    vulgaris 20
  'Granny's Bonnets 20
  seed testing 23
  the cross 21
  the seed 22
  warning 23

begonia 24–7
  assessment time 26
  Begonia lucerne 24
    rex 24
    semperflorens 24
  breeding your own 25
  final position 26
  germination 26
  sowing 25
  the seed 25

chrysanthemum 27–30, **27–9**
  China 27
  Confucius 27

Kew Gardens 27
  Order of the
    Chrysanthemum 27
  seed sowing 30
  the task 28
clematis 31–4, **32, 33**
  F2 seedlings 34
  hybridizing 31
  planting out 34
  potting on 34
  seed sowing 34

daffodils and tulips 35–8, **35–8**
  the cross 33
  the seed 37
  tulips 38
dahlias 39–42, **40–2**
  Bute, Lord 39
  Dahl 39
  Dahlia coccinea 39
    merckii 39
    variabilis 39
  Hartweg 39
  Humbolot 39
  making a start 40
  seedling selection 42
  seed sowing 41
  selection 39
delphinium 43–8, **44–8**
  Bishop, Frank 43
  Blackmore and Langdon 43
  damping off disease 46
  Delphinium cheilanthum 43
    cheilanthum 43
    elatum 43
    grandiflorum 43
    tatsienense 43
  F2 generation 48

harvest time 46
  how to make the cross 45
  Kelway 43
  'King of the Delphiniums' 43
  Lemoine 43
  'Mrs Frank Bishop' 43
  parent selection 44
  RHS show 43
  seedling development 47
  seedling selection 47
  seed sowing 46
  'Statuaire Rude' 43
  'Swan Lake' 43
  'Wrexham hybrids' 43

fuchsias 49–53, **50–3**
  crossing the flower 50
  Dominica Republic 49
  Fuchs, Leonard 49
  Fuchsia coccinea 49
    tryphilla flore coccinea 49
  Kew Gardens 49
  parental selection 50
  Plumier, Charles 49
  the flower 50
  the seed 52

gladioli 54–7, **55–7**
  back-crossing 57
  building stock 57
  Colville, G 54
  corn lilies 54
  Dioscorides 54
  Fox, Mr M. 54
  Gladioli bletchleyensis 54
    priulinus 54
  harvesting the seed 55

Hooker 54
Kelway of Langport 54
making the cross 54
planting the baby cormlets
  56
sowing the seed 56
the cross 55
gooseberry 133, **133**

hard fruits 134–7, **134–6**
  apples 134–7
  cherries 137
  colt stock, or GM9 137
  other fruits 137
  parent selection 135
  pears 137
  quince stock 137
  selection 138
  stella 137
heathers 58–62, **58–62**
  acid 58
  Calluna 58
  crossing 59
  Daboecia 58
  Erica 58
  limefree 58
  sowing the seed 61
  the cross 60
heathland berries 130
  blueberries 130
  cranberries 130

introduction 5–15, **6–15**
  fertilization 11
  flower types 7
  hay fever 9
  insect-pollinated plants 11
  modern methods 6
  outcrosses and inbreeding
    13
  parent selection 11
  plant origins 5
  pollen 7
  self-pollinating flowers 9
  wind-pollinating flowers 9
irises 63–6, **64–6**
  ancient Egyptian 63
  flag iris 63

parent selection 63
seedling selection 66
the cross 64
the seeds 65

lettuce 139
  butterhead 139
  cos 139
  crispy 139
  loose-leaved wild lettuce
    139
  prickly lettuce 139
lily 67–72, **67, 68, 70–2**
  epigeal delayed 71
  epigeal immediate 71
  growing the seed 71
  hypogeal delayed 71
  hypogeal immediate 71
  Lilium candidum 69
    chalcedonicum 69
    martagon 69
    regale **67**, 69
  Nimrod T 71
  parentage selection 69
  the cross 64
lupins 73–6, **74–6**
  better types 76
  in the greenhouse 75
  Kelway, J. 73
  Lupinus arboreus 73
    polyphyllus 73
  parental selection 73
  Russell, George 73
  seedling selection 76
  sowing the seed 75
  the best of the best 76
  the cross 74–5

pansies and violas 77–81, 77,
  79–81
  breeding 78
  dog tooth violet 77
  heartsease 77
  hybridizing brushes 79
  seedling selection 76
  seed sowing 80
  side tracking 81
  the bee at work 81

violet and violette 77
pelargonium (geranium) 82–5,
  83, 84
  cranesbill 82
  East India Company 83
  F1 hybrids 83
  next stage selection 85
  seed harvest 85
  seed sowing 85
  the cross 83
  zonals 85
phlox 86–8, **86–8**
  'Figiyama' 86
  making the cross 87
  'Omega' 86
  parental selection 87
  Phlox chatahoochee 86
    maculata 86
    panticulata 86
  sowing the seed 88
  'Starfire' 86
  the seed 88
pinks and carnations 89–94,
  89, 91, 93–4
  back crossing 94
  compost 92
  cross breeding 91
  Dianthus caryophyllus 90
  dolomite lime 92
  grit 92
  Hall, Mr Sid 90
  harvesting 92
  making a start 90
  Norman Conquest 90
  'Oakwood Crimson Clove'
    90
  seedling selection 93
  seed sowing 93
potatoes 111–14, **112, 113**
  first potatoes 114
  planting 112
  seed development 114
  selection 114
  stock selection 111
  tasting time 114
  the cross 112
primulas 95–9, **95, 97–9**
  auricula 97

Booth, J.T. 96
historical details 96
Maries, C. 96
parent selection 96
Pax System 96
pin-eye, thrum-eye 97
polyantha, primrose 96
Primulus denticulata 96
   mollis 96
   obconica 96
Royal, Dr J. Forbes 96
the seedlings 99
the seed 98

roses 100–4, **101–4**
end product 104
harvesting 103
the cross 101
the first steps 100

shrubs 140, **140**
abutilon 140
azalea 130
berberis 140
buddleia 140
cotoneaster 140

hibiscus 140
lilac (syringa) 140
potentillas 140
pyracanthas 140
strawberries 120–3, **120–3**
Fragaria chiloensis (Chilean
   strawberry) 120
   elatior (hautbois
      strawberry) 120
   vesca (wood strawberry)
      120
   virginiana (North
      American) 120
'Keens seedling' 120
'Royal Sovereign' 120
seed collection 122
the cross 121
what next 124
sweet peas 105–10 **106–9**
F1 hybrid, first generation
   110
Francis Cupani 105
germinating and growing on
   109
'Grandiflora' 105
history 105

hybridizing 106
making the cross 106
National Sweet Pea Society
   105
Ovedale, Dr 105
'Prima Donna' 105
seed sowing 108

tomatoes 115–19 **116, 118,
   119**
F1 seedlings 117
hybridizing 116
parent selection 115
seed collecting 117
seed sowing 117
the cross 116

vegetables 138
fertilizing stage 139
french beans 138
reciprocal cross 139
runner beans 138
selection 138
South American 138
the cross 138